SCHOOLMASTER SKETCHES

SCHOOLMASTER SKETCHES

BY

T. J. MACNAMARA

CASSELL AND COMPANY, LIMITED
LONDON, PARIS & MELBOURNE
1896

ALL RIGHTS RESERVED

CONTENTS.

	PAGE
A Comment	7
"Mis' Mercy"	13
Jimmy Brown	26
Sinned Against or Sinning?	42
Florrie Smith's Choice	57
By Order of the Board	95
Truly Rural	105
In the Matter of a Parchment Entry	124
Faddy, H.M.I.	142
For the Honour of the Nation	150
The Crisis at Petti-Foggerington	159
Faddy in the Girls' School	177
The Old Schoolmaster's Christmas Eve	186

A COMMENT.

IT is necessary that I should say here that every incident in the Sketches which follow has actually occurred within the past few years in connection with our State System of Elementary Schools. Many of the incidents are typical.

Thus the comments upon school work I have put into the lips of members of the Little Drivellingham, the Chewton Bunney, and other small School Boards, are only too painfully characteristic of the general attitude of the rural School Board member towards the question of Education. He doesn't believe in it; he has done splendidly—in his own estimation—without it himself; he objects to pay for it for other people's children; and he makes the life of the teacher under his sweet rule in very many cases a thing grievous to be borne. Being only human, an eighth of a penny in the pound on the rateable value of his farm is far more to him than the future of young

Hodge. So the cheaper and the nastier school work can be made, the better he is pleased.

Again, the Rev. Mr. Chittleworth, of the Church of England schools at Little Mosslington, in the story "Florrie Smith's Choice," is a gentleman to be met with only too frequently, I am sorry to say, in connection with the management of rural Voluntary schools. He considers the State School teacher *his* servant, to come and go and bring and carry just as he wills it. That, on the other hand, there are many good men of the type of "Maister Wullie," I should be grossly unjust if I did not fully and gratefully admit.

The outline of George Wooderidge's career in the same sketch is thoroughly typical of the life of the rural teacher. He has absolutely no prospect before him. Indeed, his outlook contracts as he gains experience, and as often as not he finishes up at sixty with smaller wages than he commenced with at twenty.

He holds office upon the slender tenure of a great man's nod; there is no possibility of promotion for him; and ripe experience only serves to unfit him for the slap-dash, up-to-date, grant-earning methods demanded of him.

"Faddy, H.M.I.," is admittedly overdrawn. The incidents fall thicker together in the sketch than they would do in actual life. But Faddy is, nevertheless, a very real creature, and every one of the tricks I set down against his name he has, at some time or other, been responsible for. And as for "Sneakson, H.M.I.," it would be impossible to write too harshly of him At the same time, when one considers the outrageously autocratic powers with which the "Lord Paramount" is invested, the wonder is that so many of them have acted so considerately and discriminatingly.

But whilst "Faddy" is admittedly overdrawn, it should be known to all concerned that the state of affairs described in the story "By Order of the Board" is only too genuine a picture of facts. Certain soft-hearted souls, not knowing anything about the matter, have decided that corporal punishment is bad for School Board urchins. If they could have their way in full, there would be none of this dreadful thing in the schools at all—which would be a rare thing for impudence, and worse, amongst the rising generation.

Failing to exclude it altogether, they hedge its administration round with many curious and difficult rules and regulations, and consider the teacher who infringes these in the faintest degree something a shade worse than a Thug. So children go uncorrected, and street-corners are rowdy, and magistrates and judges shake their heads in despair that things are not better "after twenty-five years of compulsory education."

The story of Emmy Page's fall from the path of rectitude illustrates the glorious absurdity of English departmental methods. Emmy knew that her Inspector would be furious on the examination day if He found in her infants' school many children over seven years of age. It was nothing to Him that the neighbourhood was poor and the parents thriftless and careless; it was nothing to Him that many children would not be driven into the school at all until eight, nine, and even ten years of age; it was nothing to Him that, even at this age, they must first pick up the rudiments in the infants' school class-room. If He found them there, their presence, in some inscrutable way, argued to Him that their teachers had been lazy, inefficient, and neglectful! So He gave everybody to understand what to expect.

Some infants' teachers solved the problem by refusing to admit the neglected seven- and eight-year-old waif; and I am not altogether sure that I blame them. Emmy Page, in her simplicity, took them all to her arms, and then, in a moment of frenzied apprehension at what would happen when Faddy came, altered several of the ages as set down in the registers from eight to seven—with the result set down in the story.

The failure of "Jimmy Brown," and the story of his attempt to missionarise in a slum school, touches the very heart of our State School system. Instead of sending Brown down into the slums to inculcate habits of cleanliness, truthfulness, and honesty amongst the forsaken little scraps entrusted to his care—doing what little he could towards book-education "in the by-going," as the Scotch say—they send him down to stand or fall professionally by his success or failure at the task of stuffing into the bewildered heads of his pitiable little charges the niceties of Parsing and Analysis, the eccentricities of our exceptional Orthography, the Gymnastics of the Decimal Point, and the height in feet of the Kinchinjunga! And this is why so much of our national expenditure on education is most sorely wasted where it is most sorely needed.

But I must not commit the unpardonable sin of moralising so early on as in my preface, or I shall defeat my purpose by losing my reader. Let me merely add that rationalisation is still sadly needed in our elementary schools, notwithstanding the splendid efforts during the past five years of Sir William Hart-Dyke and Mr. Acland, the Vice-Presidents of the Committee of Council on Education during the last Conservative and the late Liberal Administrations, and of Sir George Kekewich, the commonsense and sympathetic permanent Secretary at the Education Office.

That this rationalisation may be secured, I have, as a variant upon urging the matter from the public platform, written these Sketches, setting out in fictional form the facts underlying the truth about our method of controlling Elementary Education. Several of them have appeared in the columns of the *Schoolmaster*, and to the Directors of that journal I am indebted for the permission to reproduce the same.

If I can only lure the reading public into a perusal of these stories, and thereby into a passing interest in the Education Question—for I am regretfully compelled to acknowledge that the public interest in the matter is not a thing to strike attitudes over, always excepting, of course, the religious phase of the problem, the necessity for discussing which I have ventured to gauge by declining to pen a single syllable on it—I shall be more than satisfied that good will accrue.

T. J. MACNAMARA.

LONDON, 1896.

SCHOOLMASTER SKETCHES

"MIS' MERCY."

You see, they train them so much better nowadays. At all the best colleges they give them a rare course of two years' theoretical school method of the most delightful kind. Psychology is studied; Herbert Spencer turned inside out for all he is worth. Good old John Locke is nowhere. Pestalozzi and Froebel are all the vogue. And so the young schoolmistresses go down to take charge of the rural schools perfect geniuses of the science and art of diagnosing and developing the child mind.

Only, and notwithstanding recent fine endeavours at reform, the Government methods of measuring up their work are still terribly square-toed; and some of the men appointed to test their labours still terribly incapable of recognising the value of anything beyond the mere mechanical.

So all their fine theories are knocked out of them within the first month, and then they go back to the rough-and-ready methods of their old pupil-teacher days, and good examinations are passed, rich grants are earned, Government Inspectors smile, and school managers send resolutions of congratulation!

That is, if they recover the shock; for two years' dallying with Arnold and Thring gives ideas from which it is a bit of a wrench to part. Some fail to recover themselves. They fight tenaciously for the newer, the more human, and the more educational way. These are they who, after a brief and unavailing struggle against the Stolidity of the Established Rule, go under and pass out into the bitterness reserved for those who fail.

Now "Mis' Mercy" was one of these last, for undoubtedly "Mis' Mercy" was a failure.

Cobbler Maggs has passed judgment, so there was nothing more to be said.

"Mis' Mercy," I ought to say, came down to Little Drivellingham nearly two years ago from the Royal Normal College for the Training of Village Schoolmistresses. Up to the time of her coming, the school had achieved wonders in the way of scoring marvellous percentages at the Government examinations. If Miss Driver, the previous mistress, couldn't make the quotient touch ninety-seven per cent. in the absorbing calculation she invariably entered upon directly the schedules giving the results of her pupils' struggles on the examination day came under her eager gaze, then the little Drivellinghamites knew it. And when the percentage system met with a well-deserved fate, Miss Driver actually cried for vexation!

Mind you, I am not blaming Miss Driver. Promotion to a more congenial sphere, and emancipation from the deadly dreariness of village life, were only open to her through " clean " schedules;* and " clean " schedules she meant to have, whoever suffered.

Unfortunately, her work was tested by an Inspector to whom the spelling of cider with an *s* meant so much laziness and malingering on the part of the teacher. Hence Miss Driver—very wisely, from her own point of view—laid herself out to anticipate My Lord Paramount's wishes to a nicety, thereby winning great renown for herself and the highest possible grants for the members of her School Board.

So everybody—save possibly the children and their parents, in whose minds was at least one serious reservation—voted her the best teacher the village had ever known; and when she secured the mistress-

---

* "CLEAN" SCHEDULES.—The "Schedule" is the list of the scholars presented to the Inspector for examination. When not disfigured with " 0's," recording failure on the part of the pupil in one or other of the subjects of examination, the schedule, in teaching parlance, is styled " clean."

ship of a fine new Board School in the neighbouring county town, it was, by something like common consent, agreed that it would be hard indeed to fill Miss Driver's place.

And undoubtedly "Mis' Mercy" had been a failure.

Let me tell you about her. Perhaps I can best give you in a word an indication of the sort of girl Mercy Hope was when I say that all the girls at the College loved her. You know what *that* means. You know what a searching test of Character is the little Republic of College life; and you know how absolutely unfailing are its judgments. Mercy Hope was easily the most universally loved girl of her year. Had you the toothache? Mercy was the first to sympathise. Was it a cup of tea in bed? Sure as to-morrow's sun it would be Mercy's hand that would brew it and smooth out the crumpled pillow while you drank it. Was it a letter from Jack? Whom to confide in but Mercy? And if the girls wanted a favour of the dear old Lady Superintendent, whom so likely to charm consent as Mercy?

Well, Mercy had gone to Little Drivellingham to take Miss Driver's place, and the long and the short of the matter was, Mercy had failed; failed ignominiously.

My Lord Paramount—by whom I mean, of course,

the Government Inspector—had noted with extreme regret in the Report after Mercy's first six months, that there was a very serious falling-off in the mechanical results. A sort of blight had smitten the nimble intellects of the little Drivellinghamites. Their writing was scarcely so uniformly clean, or so perfectly regular as heretofore; they grappled with the intricacies of our exceptional orthography far less satisfactorily than at previous examinations; yes, indeed, for the first time within the history of the school, Mr. Faddy, the Inspector, found youngsters of seven not able to distinguish between the use of *there* and *their* in the spelling tests! And, as a matter of fact, one scandalously careless imp of eight had actually dared to write the dictated phrase "*The clothes they wear*" thus: "*The close thay ware*"! Even more, will it be believed, some of the infants had actually worked their straightforward sums inaccurately!

All this was strangely new in this particular school, and My Lord Paramount shrewdly summed up the situation in his own mind. However, for the time being, he simply regretted the falling-of; described it as due, no doubt, to the changes in the staff; gave notice that this was a case where he must certainly perpetuate the annual examination; and hoped to see things as of old when he should come again next year.

To say that Mercy's sensations were a trifle mixed as she sat over the fire in the footy little front room at her lodgings at the close of the day of the Inspector's first annual visit is to put the matter far more mildly than perhaps the situation demands. She was simply bewildered and in a maze.

What had she done? Had she been lazy? Indifferent? Thoughtless?

Nay, the very reverse was nearer the truth. Her school and her little charges had been her one engrossing care from the first night when she had unstrapped her box in the cottage of the rector's gardener.

She had found the children heavy, listless, mechanical, and devoid of a single interest when once inside the four walls of the village school. They would read with the letter-perfect readiness of a phonograph, spell like Noah Webster, and total up strings of figures in a way that would have charmed Babbage himself. They out-parroted the best-trained parrot that ever came across sea. But of everything not included in the Syllabus of the Subjects of Instruction set out in the Government Code of Regulations they were stupendously ignorant. Of the teeming phenomena of nature all round them, the growing hedgerow, changing season, winds and their portent, life in its multitude of forms — of these things, I say, Mercy's pupils seemed to know but little, and that darkly.

So she took pity upon them in the fulness of her human sympathy and interest. She taught them to see, to hear, and to understand. School-time, which had in the past been for them a howling waste, dry, hard, and unlovely, now blossomed under the tender hand of a loving woman into a sweet and profitable vale, full of attraction, loveliness, and sweet remembrance.

And it was because of this, and the eternal stupidity of Things Administrative, that after six months' toil she sat before the fire at her lodgings, her eyelids smarting and a big tear welling down a hot and flushed face.

As for the future, the disheartened girl saw, after much peering into the fire, the faintest gleam of hope upon the horizon of her despairful outlook. Maybe after another year the fruits of her fuller, more human, and more intelligent teaching would tell, and then all would be well. So she would bravely face another year and struggle on.

Well, that year of toil and endeavour had come and gone; and Mercy had failed. My Lord Paramount had been shocked at the continued falling-off in mechanical accuracy. Miss Hope was obviously "weak." True, there was a touch of greater intelligence in the children's answering, but the whole thing was so wofully lacking in precision, smartness, and examination precocity. The "results" had not been attained. Grants must fall to the lowest limits, and the Board must be warned that "unless greater improvement was shown next year," etc. etc., "My Lords of the Committee of Council on Education would be compelled," and so on and so on.

And from Board Member and Inspector went up with one voice the announcement of Mercy's failure.

Ten days since, the School Board had met and called upon her to resign—young Farmer Fowler dissenting—and Cobbler Maggs, in his nightly part of village oracle, was especially great that evening in the Bar Parlour of "The Plough" upon the question of her failings.

"A course er've a done bad at the 'xamination! A course, I says! 'Ow cood'ee exspeck otherwise? Wy! I 'ears as 'ow her do go a gallivantin' down the lanes with the childern nigh on every arternoon a-pickin' up leaves an' gumming 'em in books, an' makin' the childern tell their names an' all that nonsense!"

"Ees!" chimed in Farmer Cann, another member

of the School Board; "an' I 'ears as 'ow she've a got a stuffed owl in the schule, and sum wite mice! 'Er do spend 'ole 'ours a-tellin' 'em about clouds and airy-mouzes an' 'edge'ogs an' black-biddels! Did'ee ever 'ear a such rot?"

"Bah! that ain't the worst on it," gurgled Sleeman, his nose half inside a pewter mug. "Ev'ee never seed that glass thing-a-me-jig in the winder?"

Some had, some hadn't.

"Well," continued Sleeman, with the air of a man about to communicate the finishing-touch to Information, "Well, wat do'ee think 'er keeps in un?"

"Lord knaws!" was the general character of the reply.

"Well, I'll tell'ee. Er've a got that glass thing aaf filled wi' watter; an' in the watter er've a got noots, an' lizurds, an' toewuds, an' frogs! Ees! Gospel!" added Sleeman, in response to the look of incredulity on every face.

The first man to break the silence was Jan Tucker, who, after confessing himself as thoroughly and effectually damned, went on to say that the sooner she left the village the better, and to describe how he had gone into the school one day for his little Billy, and had found the said Billy "playin' wi' mud pies, and makin' apples out of clay!"

So, as the clock was striking ten, the village parliament shook itself together and toddled off home in various directions and by devious paths, the universal agreement being that Mercy Hope was a sham and a fraud.

And so it had come about that Mercy had failed, and was to go home in disgrace. How *that* affected her I need not essay to tell you. What she wrote to the old people I don't know: but I know it wrung the very heart's blood from her to write it.

She had scarcely begun to make preparations for her departure two months distant; but every morning, when she met her children anew, a glistening eye here and a touch of demonstrative affection there reminded her that her last day as mistress in the village school was slipping nigher and nigher.

Then a dreadful thing happened. Always shockingly insanitary in its condition, Little Drivellingham had suffered terribly in the cholera plague of the 'Fifties, as the churchyard record showed. Epidemics among the children were so common as to go unnoticed. There never was a time when some family or other was not down with measles, scarlatina, mumps, or something else. And were it not that God's air is fresh and the countryside broad and open, the insanitary condition of the little village would long since have wiped it out of existence.

Just before the time came for "Mis' Mercy" to leave, diphtheria broke out badly among the villagers, and especially rapid was its spread amongst the children. The school was closed six weeks before Mercy's term of notice expired. They paid her off, and told her she might leave at once.

But she didn't. Every cottage in the village was a hospital ward so far as the presence of a prostrate patient was concerned; but the other attributes—trained nursing, alleviating medicines, and nourishing foods—were sorely wanting. And Mercy Hope stayed on, passing from sickroom to sickroom, an angel of love, beneficence, and solicitude.

Many of the villagers died—many of the children. But many others owe their existence to-day to the loving kindness and care of the schoolmistress who failed.

And the chairman and the clerk of the School Board, when things began to get a bit straight, met together to draft the advertisement for the new mistress.

But they never drafted it. For Tanner, the chairman, told the clerk that he'd see himself—well, never mind what—before he'd sign it, and gave it out that he intended to get the Board to ask Miss Hope to withdraw her resignation and continue in the school.

Which is exactly what the Board did at its next meeting, without a single dissentient. And young Tom Fowler, who had always had a sneaking regard for the pretty little mistress, left the Board at once to hurry off and convey the news to Mercy Hope at her lodgings.

Eager as you like, he tied his horse to the gateway at the rector's gardener's, and knocked loud enough almost to give Mrs. Jenkins a fit.

"Mis' Hope in?" shouted young Tom.

"Yes, sir," replied Mrs. Jenkins, in a half-tearful, half-broken voice, "I'm sorry to say she is. As you know, she hasn't laid down upon her bed this three weeks, and last night Dr. Bond brought her home too ill to stand. She's been in bed ever since." And here Mrs. Jenkins broke down utterly.

Gathering herself together after a moment or two, she added, amidst her sobs: "And oh! Mr. Tom! *She's got it!*"

"Mis' Mercy" had caught the diphtheria at last. Little wonder. And in her present exhausted state her chances of recovery were almost *nil* from the beginning.

That night the clerk of the Board sent by hand the formal written resolution of the Board, cordially asking her to withdraw her resignation. Hours they had spent over it, trying to turn it out nicely worded, and to make it in some measure an expression of opinion suited to the occasion.

It was the last thing Mercy Hope understood on this side of the grave.

They took it, blurred and crumpled, from her locked fingers before another sun had sped its course.

A week later, if you had chanced across the little village, you would have felt a mighty hush, even in the air of heaven. And no birds seemed to sing. The very bell in the belfry tower seemed to have caught an added touch of grief and melancholy, whilst from the graveyard behind the church there was borne upon the air a slow and pathetic hymn, chanted in a quivering key to the last tune Mercy had taught her charges at the village school.

There, midst the many newly-made, mean-looking graves and heaped-up mounds of red clodded earth, is one marked by no monumental tablet; for friends are poor, and there are the living to keep alive. But embedded in its surface are jars and glasses from many a cottage sideboard, and each holds a profusion of newly-plucked flowers, so that no trace of the red earth is seen—the red earth that covers all that remains of the mere obscure village schoolmistress who failed.

JIMMY BROWN.

"I SAY, chaps!"—ay, we were "chaps" once more, although above the ears there were sprinklings of grey—"I say, chaps! does any of ye know what became of Jimmy Brown?"

It was Whit-Monday and the annual College reunion. The young bloods were yelling their heads off, running their heats, jumping their hurdles, and wriggling themselves through ludicrously artificial "obstacles" to an alarming accompaniment of strange and disquieting cries, amongst which "Bravo, Arcadia!" "What price Demons *now!*" and "Good lad, Legs!" linger in my memory by reason of their utter unintelligibility.

A half-dozen of us, 'Seventy-nine and 'Eighty men, had foregathered under the shade at the bottom of the cricket-field to talk over days lang syne, and—"Does any of ye know what became of Jimmy Brown?" was the question in Seebohm's still cheery and still unconventional tones.

"Jimmy Brown? Ah, my boys, he was the pick

of the covey after all, wasn't he?" Thus Andrew Merrifield; and we all assented with profound agreement.

For a moment silence followed. We were thinking of Jimmy Brown, his prowess in the football field, his deeds in the "Gym," and his unquenchable good-nature and warm-heartedness.

"Jimmy," by common consent, had been indeed "the pick of the covey" in that little republic where sterling manliness and true grit alone win distinction. And probably most of us were thinking too, at the moment, that if there *was* a man amongst the fifty-five of us that lived through those magic years '79 and '80 together who *ought* to have forged his way in the world beyond all others, Jimmy was the man.

At last Dick Marks broke the silence.

"Jimmy Brown?" said Marks slowly and contemplatively, poising a foul-looking briar between his thumb and first two fingers—Marks smoked even at College, and used to make boast of the practice of striking his vestas on the stone framework of the front doorway as he went out, much to the terror and bewilderment of the juniors in their very early days—"Jimmy Brown? Yes, I can tell you what became of him, up to a certain point, at any rate."

"Well, what? Go ahead!"

"Don't get excited," drawled the imperturbable Marks, "or I shall dry up!"

"Sorry, old man," chimed in the Irrepressible; "*go ahead!*"

"Well, Jimmy went back to Tykington—he was a P.T. there, you know—as an assistant. He got on A1, I believe, and then got a crib as headmaster at Ironden, about the first in our year, I think, who *got* a good headship."

"So far, I think, we all know," broke in Lumley. "I remember seeing *that* in the '84 'Year-Book.'"

"Well, Jimmy's school was in a terribly poor neighbourhood. The School Board was outside the borough, and one and all of 'em made big grants the one purpose of the teacher's existence. I sometimes think now there was a bit of excuse for 'em. The rateable value——"

"Here, dry up, Marks! You're not addressing an N. U. T.* meeting, you know!"

It was the Irrepressible again, and Marks turned his head sharply and struck his favourite attitude, pipe militant this time.

Dick Marks, you must know, had gained renown

---

* The N. U. T., it is perhaps necessary to say, is the National Union of Teachers, a powerfully-organised body, having for its aims the advancement of Popular Education and the safeguarding of the status of the teacher.

as a leader of the Teachers' Union, and was big on educational politics.

"No, old man," he went on, as the momentary hardness died out of his face, and then, as if Seebohm's interruption had been sufficiently "squashed"—to use one of the old terms—in the magnificence of his scornful glance, he repeated slowly, "the—rateable—value, as I was saying, was extremely low, a penny in the pound bringing in something like £250"—[Seebohm inwardly groaned, a grumbling, if hopeless protest]—"whilst inside the borough a penny in the pound brought in £5,000. So, you see, as the rates were fearfully high, there was some excuse for these fellows insisting upon the highest grants. Now, of course, the *remedy* would have been——"

"Here, I *must* object *this* time," again broke in Seebohm. "*Hang* yer remedies; this is Whit-Monday and the Re-union. What we want to know is *what became of Jimmy Brown!*" And we one and all thought the Irrepressible had right on his side, *this* time at any rate.

"Oh, very well, chaps," gently assented Marks, "all right. Hang the remedy. So be it. Well, to make a long story short, Jimmy resented from the beginning this grant-grinding craze. The first week he was in the school he took all his fellows aside, and insisted that they should one and all take the screw off.

"They helplessly shook their heads and thought of their own positions at the end of the year, and the rises of screw that were styled 'automatic' in the Board's scale as one of the many pleasant figments for which the clerk of the Board had been responsible.

"Jimmy told his staff to leave everything to him. He would bear the brunt of whatever censure followed. And for the remaining six months of the school-year Urchin Alley became a real centre of true educational work. I know exactly how Jimmy went to work, because he told me himself many times afterwards at Tykington when he came home for his holidays to see the old people and his sweetheart.

"First of all, he organised a general morning wash. Then he issued the most terrifically awe-inspiring rules against obscene writing either in the reading-books or on the walls. Next he taught the youngsters himself how to play. Yes; how to play —I remember him giving me a really pathetic description of how they used to hang about the playground at playtime and in the dinner-hour, simply powerless to amuse themselves. Telling lies and deceit of any form he was down upon like a thousand bricks, as you may imagine.

"As to the school work, I know he told me that he absolutely took away and locked up fifteen packs of arithmetic test cards his Standard IV. teacher was scientifically and systematically putting the boys through; and tore up no end of books of tests on all sorts of subjects set in previous years by the Inspectors. They were going to *missionarise* first of all, Jimmy told his staff, and after that they were going to *teach* in a really humanising and pleasant fashion.

"Cramming up for the exam. Jimmy wouldn't hear of; and all the thousand and one expedients, carefully collected for many years by Jimmy's predecessor, in order to bring things to the highest state of French polish upon the examination day, Jimmy put out of sight on the top shelf of his cupboard once and for all."

"Jimmy was a fool," quoth Charlie Smedley, interrupting, and probably most of us thought very much as Charlie did.

"Fool or no fool," continued Dick, "this is exactly what happened."

"Well," added Smedley, "tell us what happened at the exam."

"Several things," sententiously replied Marks. "First of all there was a deuce of a row over the

Exemption List*—it was before its abolition of course, as you know; and if ever there was——"

"Ahem!" coughed the Irrepressible, showing a smiling set of teeth.

"Thanks, old man," muttered our narrator, sinking back into his accustomed repose of manner, and replacing the pipe.

"Well, not to worry you with any reflections on the matter, I will simply say again that it was in the days of the Exemption Schedule.

"Now Jimmy had made up his list on the Saturday night previous to the Monday morning of the

---

* THE "EXEMPTION" LIST.—When an Inspector paid his annual visit of examination to a school, the teacher was permitted to enter upon an "Exemption" List the names of such children as might reasonably be excused the ordeal of examination on the ground of physical or mental unfitness, and so on. S me Inspectors objected most strongly to this list if it contained more than one or two names per hundred of the pupils, with the result that great over-pressure ensued, and in some cases children not likely to shine on the Parade Day found it a trifle difficult to get into a school at all. One of the most grotesque features about the whole business was the fact that irregularity of attendance was held to be no reason for the exceptional treatment of a child on the examination day. Teachers were thus driven well-nigh to desperation at the pleasant task of trying to make bricks without straw. Another of the charming ways of the system was this: that once a child's name was put on the Exemption Schedule he could not then, under any power in Heaven or earth, be *examined*. If the reason for the presence of his name on the "Exemption" List was a good one, the Inspector wrote "E" upon the Schedule, and all was well. If, however, the reason was, in his opinion, *not* a good one, then he wrote "N E" upon the form, *and the child was counted, to the teacher's professional detriment, a failure in all the subjects of examination*. . Oh! it was a glorious system.

examination. One of the boys in it was down as 'In custody.' He had been milking a dairyman's cow into his hat earlier in the week. Jimmy had understood that he would remain in custody at any rate until the following Friday. When, lo and behold! the first thing that met Jimmy's eye on arriving at the school this auspicious Monday morning was this precious boy outside the door, his ear this time in custody, the custodian being his father.

"Explanations followed, and Jimmy took the young man inside.

"Ten o'clock brought the Inspectors, Wragge the Sub, and two assistants. Wragge was an unhappy example, I grant you, of the system of selecting very young teachers to become H.M. Inspector's Assistants and ultimately Subs; but of course the principle is as sound as a——"

(Seebohm had emitted just the faintest preliminary to a deprecatory cough, and Marks, admitting the impeachment, nodded reassuringly and continued.)

"Well, Wragge and Jimmy tackled the Exemption List first of all, and after a common agreement upon the first three names, came to the case of the youngster marked down as 'in custody.'

"'This is the case of a boy,' explained Jimmy, 'who got into trouble last week for securing a free drink for himself by milking one of Chalk's cows, grazing in the Church fields, into his hat. He was in custody when I made up the list late on Saturday night, and I understood he would remain in custody till the weekly petty sessions next Friday. However, he turned up this morning, and here he is.'

"'Dear me,' minced Wragge; 'how peculiar! What do you suggest, Mr. Brown?'

"'Well, I think we might strike his name off *this* list now he's here, and let him go to his class and take his chance,' said Jimmy.

"'Wait a moment; wait a moment; not so fast, Mr. Brown, *if* you please,' replied Wragge in his best judicial style.

"'Now let me *see*. In the *first* place, if his name is on the Exemption Schedule I cannot examine him. That is point number *one*. If the reason for the presence of his name on this list is a *good* one, I write "*E*" on the schedule, and the matter is at an end; point number *two*. If the reason for the presence of his name on this list,' toying it fondly with his blue lead, 'is er—a—er *bad one*, then I write "*N E*" on the schedule, and again the matter is at an end; point number *three*. See, Mr. Brown?'

"'But surely, Mr. Wragge,' blurted out Jimmy, 'in the name of common sense you are not going to——'

"'Nay, Mr. Brown,' gently insisted Wragge, 'not so fast, not so fast. It is not a matter of common sense; it is a matter of carrying out my regulations, any deviation from which you, I do not doubt, would be the first to resent.' (Wragge scored here, for Jimmy had been slipping into the Inspectors at a recent teachers' meeting.)

"'But, Mr. Wragge,' expostulated Jimmy, his dander getting up.

"'*Gently*, Mr. Brown. You may leave this to me. Now let me apply my three points to this interesting case,' went on Wragge in the most exasperating fashion. 'In the *first* place, I am absolutely precluded from *examining* this boy. That is settled. The presence of his name in this list decides *that*. Now let us see if your reason is a good one, in which case I will write "*E*" after his name upon the schedule with pleasure. You say he is "in custody"?'

"'Well, he was when I made up the list,' blurted out Jimmy, nearly at the end of his patience.

"'Nay, nay. Here am I this morning, 4th November, 10.15 a.m., face to face with your reason, "In custody," and'—this with fine rhetorical effort, pointing towards the boy at Jimmy's side—'there, *there is the boy!* No, Mr. Brown; "*N E*," *if* you please, and three noughts upon the schedule!'

"'Well, I'm——' muttered Jimmy, checking himself suddenly, scarlet in the face and boiling with rage.

"But Wragge went on. 'Now let us take your fifth case.'

"For a moment Jimmy thought of telling him bluntly to do what he liked with the rest. But second thoughts prevailed, and on he went with Wragge through that miserable Exemption List. And Jimmy had made it a long one, you bet. That was his line; a line, no doubt, that had set Wragge against him from the first, for Jimmy told me that he pulled a face as long as a fiddle directly he looked at it.

"By-and-by they came to the cases of two brothers, against each of whose names Jimmy had the statement 'No clothes.' That, of course, was a fact. Father and mother were thriftless, dissolute wretches, and the house was literally empty. The two boys, as Jimmy knew from personal inquiry, were fighting November's fog and cold upon an old mattress, covered with some sacking the neighbours had lent them.

"'*No clothes!*' broke out Wragge, in an air of superlative astonishment. 'I *can't* pass *that*. I shall have nothing but "No clothes" all over the district if I do!'

"'Well,' said Jimmy, with that queer look in the corner of his eye that meant mischief on the football field to the half-back coming flying down towards him, 'Well, what do you propose to do?'

"'Propose to *do!*' answered Wragge, 'Why, write "*N E*" after both!'

"'Oh dear no, you won't,' said Jimmy quietly. 'We'll have *this* thing, at any rate, settled on a logical basis!'

"'Wha'?' said Wragge, aghast.

"'*Yes*,' replied Jimmy steadily. 'Here, Mr. Long'—this to one of his assistants standing nearest—'take my overcoat, and get Mr. Emery to go with you with his; run round to 19, Hill Street; you'll find the two Smiths in the front room downstairs, naked. Wrap 'em up—stay; better take a couple of overcoats—and bring 'em down. We'll have *these* two examined, anyhow, even if we have to do it naked.' And Jimmy strolled away from Wragge, as his two assistants made for the door."

"Wragge didn't get much change out of Jimmy *that* time," interpolated the Irrepressible.

"You're right," replied Marks, warming up to his subject; "but let me finish.

"Wragge was staggered for a moment. Then recovering himself, he blurted out, 'Oh—er—Mr.

Brown—er—one moment, if you please; call your assistants back!'

"'No, *Sir*,' said Jimmy, now thoroughly roused, 'call 'em back yourself if you want 'em!'

"Of course this was open mutiny. And Wragge threw up his hands in horror. 'Do—I—understand—you—to—say—Mr. Brown'—and he bit the words out with lips white with anger, 'that you won't *obey* me?'

"'You do, sir,' said Jimmy.

"'Then perhaps,' said Wragge, recovering himself and turning to Mr. Tapes, one of his assistants, '*you*, Mr. Tapes, will fetch those two young men back.'

"Which Mr. Tapes did, of course."

"Well, what then?" asked Mr. Seebohm eagerly.

"Oh, well," continued Marks, "Wragge said he would have to take the most serious notice of the incident, and then the exam. went on.

"Everything went wrong, naturally. Would have done in *any* case, even if the trouble over the Exemption Schedule had not arisen. The fine gloss which Wragge and his colleagues had been accustomed to look for was absent. As I told you, Jimmy would have none of it. And in the end the school passed an atrociously bad exam. If Wragge had had half an eye he would have seen, of course, how much happier the boys were than in previous years, how little of feverish anxiety there was amongst them, how much more genuinely healthy the whole thing was. But perhaps the Exemption Schedule incident blurred his vision a bit.

"At any rate, when the report came back ten weeks later—Jimmy's parchment, I may tell you, had not yet been returned to him—the Board held a special committee at the school to inquire into things. All the lower grants were given. They lost the grant for grammar entirely, and the report was a scorcher. Poor old Jimmy spent a bad afternoon that day, I can tell you. The chairman of the committee sanctimoniously expressed their extreme pain at the inexcusable falling-off in the efficiency of the school—falling-off of grants he meant, of course—and formally warned Jimmy that far different things would be expected next year. Indeed, it was only because he had been there but six months that they hesitated in recommending more serious steps *immediately* to the Board, &c. &c.

"Jimmy heard it all in silence, offered no explanation, uttered no excuse. But what knocked him most was when they came to this sentence in the report, and asked for an explanation:—

"'*My Lords regret to have to say that unless*

Mr. Brown's manner towards H.M. Inspector undergoes a material improvement, My Lords will be compelled to suspend his certificate.

"'*Meanwhile, pending the forwarding to Mr. Brown of his parchment certificate, My Lords will be glad to hear that Mr. Brown has apologised to H.M. Sub-Inspector Mr. Wragge for the incidents which transpired upon the first day of the annual examination, Monday, 4th November.*'

"Jimmy laughed a sort of aimless, helpless laugh, and rambled out some explanation or other, and then went downstairs from the cookery room, in which the committee met, to his school——" and Marks paused for a moment in the recountal of his long story.

"Well, well! what then?" several of us were asking in chorus.

"Well, fact is, I don't exactly know what happened then," replied Dick.

"All I know is, that Jimmy went up to Wragge's house that night with a copy of the part of the report I've told you of with him. They had about three minutes together in Wragge's front room, and Wragge had to cancel all further inspection engagements for six weeks, during which time he wasn't seen out of doors!"

"By Jove!" muttered Lumley. "And what of Jimmy?"

"Jimmy!" answered Marks. "Oh, Jimmy is an engine-driver now, I believe, up in North-West India."

SINNED AGAINST OR SINNING?

Now, I am not going to attempt a justification of fraud. And if I were, these would be the last pages in which I should essay the task. For all that, I make bold to ask the question in the line which serves as the title of my story; and I am not sure that at its close the replies will all be condemnatory.

* * * * *

Emmy and I first struck up a friendship at College six years ago, where she had been my "daughter," as we styled it. As her senior I was, of course, responsible for her proper upbringing, and a more sweet-tempered, delightfully-dispositioned disciple I could not have wished.

Everybody loved Emmy, and in return she loved everybody. Little children were especially her delight; and how the infants in the Practising School loved her! But I must stay my pen, or Emmy's praises will occupy me to the end.

Of course, she was not without her faults. I think she was a wee bit vain—and well she might be. And no doubt those hard, shrewd natures who set up a rigid standard for themselves and all the world would have told you that Emmy was a wofully weak little thing. Miss Sterne, our S.M. lecturer, I know, thought so. Nor did she spare Emmy plenty of "thoroughly good talks," designed to effect the most salutary changes in her will-power, talks which only left my little one with burning eyelids, and more helpless than before.

Well, to make a long story short—for I have no heart to elaborate details—Emmy came to the school where I had already been installed a year, on leaving College, and it is perhaps not necessary to say that we lodged together.

The work was cruelly hard for both of us—I in the girls' department, and Emmy in the Infants'. Large classes, poor, half-clad, shivering little bits of humanity—and an eternal grind, grind, grind, from the doughy bread and weak tea of the cheap, dreary little parlour in the morning, to the doughy bread and weak tea of the still more dreary little parlour in the night. Oh, it was a cursed tragedy of existence—hard, solitary, and smileless.

Yes, we went to the N. U. T. meetings, but there everybody seemed to be squabbling. The master of our school, Mr. Mendment, especially posed as the

Ishmaelite of the proceedings; and he was always good for a row, failing other causes for dissension, about some alleged ancient misallocation of a guinea raised for the Benevolent Funds after a big social tea somewhere about the year 1879, as far as I could gather.

But Mr. Mendment very rarely had to fall back upon this hoary feud in default of more topical grounds for dissension. At the meetings we attended —for we struggled hard to realise and act up to our instinctive conceptions of professionalism—the whole well-being of the English educational system seemed to hang upon the decision whether or not something or other called "Electoral Districts" should be introduced into the domestic machinery of the Union. I could never make out what it really meant; as for Emmy, I usually had to take her home directly after tea with a dreadful headache.

I know it is very wrong of me not to idealise our N. U. T. meetings. I feel I ought to. I am still a member, and always shall be—as I hope every girl is or will be. But oh! I *do* wish the meetings were more really interesting and attractive to us tired, disenchanted, and ofttimes thoroughly heart- and home-sick girls.

Yes, and we went in for two sciences each,

magnetism and physiology, and spent hours and hours over the third-grade freehand, to say nothing of the painting class at the institute and a weekly choir practice at the chapel. So, you see, our time was well filled up.

Had it not been, Mrs. Jones's little front parlour: the yellow gauze around the picture-frames; the print of the Descent of the Dove, hideous even to the limit of positive profanity; the sticky armchair, with its contumacious horse-hair stuffing, its broken seat-spring, its missing castor, and its wobbly arm; all these, terrible at night in their mocking obliviousness to the all-pervading oiliness of the paraffin lamp, would have sent me, at any rate, stark staring mad many a time.

As for Emmy, she got on admirably. She loved her children, and tried her best to love her work. But, true to that instinct of real sympathy with the little ones which formed the striking characteristic in her nature, she was always in open warfare against many of the regulations which shackled her hands and crushed her spirit.

At the first examination—the one at which I got my much-prayed-for parchment — she learnt several things that were as a revelation to her.

I know she came home burningly furious and

indignant against the great Faddy about a lesson he had given her in needle drill, amongst other things.

But what struck dismay and disgust into her usually placid temperament was a circumstance with which she was not directly connected or concerned.

Miss Brown, the headmistress, was a curious mixture of kindliness and Codal cruelty. Yes, cruelty. There is no softer word for it. Take Miss Brown as a woman, you found a kindly, sympathetic nature, and this continued so long as you could keep the thought of the Code out of her mind. But all at once she would, as it were, start as if with remorse at her own weakness, put on the professional exterior, look set and hard, and then you saw only the brilliantly successful Code-grinder. The needs of the children became immediately subordinated to their possibilities of achievement as units on the examination day. The sympathetic instinct of the woman struggled momentarily with the professionalist, able to wring out the highest variable grant and the very best report in the district. But the struggle was only momentary, and it was not the womanly instinct which prevailed.

Well, the school was in a wretched neighbourhood. Want and poverty were the dread accompaniments of the daily lives of all the children—crime and drink of many. And, as every teacher knows, schoolwork in such a district is a penal servitude not known of My Lords of Whitehall. If Miss Brown could have been unchained from the Code, and set free to missionarise as her womanly feelings directed, some lasting benefit might have been conferred upon all connected with the work. As it was, there was the same terror of the Annual Ordeal, and the same footrule to measure up the work, that now and then worried and tried the teacher even in the West-End School.

Yet Miss Brown forgot herself now and again—especially when some barefooted, towsly-haired urchin was driven into school over six years of age. For a while Miss Brown would try hard to wheedle, argue, or cajole Mr. Timms and my mistress, Miss Totts—the heads of the boys' and girls' schools—into agreement to take these neglected waifs into the Boys' or Girls' Departments. If they should be found in the Infants' School over seven years of age on the examination day, Faddy would pull a face as long as a fiddle and kick up no end of a fuss. Miss Brown knew this from bitter experience. And yet the attitude taken up by Mr. Timms and Miss Totts was an eminently reasonable one. These children couldn't say their letters—didn't know B from a bull's foot, in short. The infants' school was their proper place, and into the infants' school they went, after a final remonstrance from Miss Brown.

And it was by reason of their presence that Emmy came home from school in a terror of dismay and disgust, as I have already said. Faddy had waxed furious when he found there were twenty-two children in the school over seven. You might plead with him until patience itself revolted, about their previously neglected condition, and you would plead in vain. It was nothing to him that they had not come to school at all until seven itself nearly. That was a matter for which the School Board was somehow or other mysteriously responsible. It was nothing to him that they knew absolutely nothing on admission, and couldn't very well be taught their letters in the upper departments. He pooh-poohed all that. He would deal with the matter in the Report; and he should on no account think of awarding the Higher Grant.

And so Miss Brown and all her staff went home with red eyes and bitterly disappointed spirits, and for a long time Faddy's name seemed a synonym for a variety of ugly terms, of which perhaps "Brute" and "Beast" were the most frequently requisitioned.

"But," said Miss Brown, directly her professionalism reasserted itself, "never no more! Never no more! They shall run the streets first."

How that may be I don't know; but this I *do* know—that things never went more swimmingly in the infants' school than at the next two examinations.

So time went on, and Emmy and I plodded on—smiling now, grumbling then, never quite disheartened, often as merry as sandboys. And how we revelled in the Midsummer holidays! For two years running we went together to Emmy's home at Oakappleton, in Devonshire, and snatched an all-too-brief three weeks from fairyland. Mr. and Mrs. Page were passionately attached to their only daughter, as many tins of cream and many more letters from home had already taught me. But it was not until I had gone with Emmy to her home that I realised the measure of their affection.

Then came a step up for Emmy, who was appointed by the Board to open a new infants' school across the river in quite as poor a part as ours. Her joy at having a school of her own, and her genuine solicitude for the slowness of promotion in my own case, scarce need the telling. Neither is it necessary to say that she threw herself into her new work with an energy that knew no relaxing. But it was a cruel task. The neighbourhood was not only as poor as ours, but it had never before had a school in its midst. What happens to the teachers then, only those who have gone through the trial can tell you. Emmy's children when driven into school usually cried or screamed, according to their ages, for the first three days. They were dirty even to the extent of filthiness, and more closely resembled a pen of newly-captured young wild animals than anything else I can think of.

However, she stood up bravely to her task, and if she wrung her hands occasionally of a night at home in our lodgings—for we still lived together—I do not doubt that she felt the more relieved thereby for her next day's struggle.

One matter troubled her sorely. As might have been expected, she was compelled to admit a really alarming number of children over six years of age. Turn them away she would not, although visions of Miss Brown made their admission seem almost to her simple mind in the nature of a crime. How she worried over them! And how she lacerated herself with rehearsals of the scenes with Faddy.

This matter, I know, drove her very nearly beside herself as the examination day loomed near, and I had a heavy task before me to chaff her out of her stupidity. I failed in my effort, and Emmy got more and more worried and scared, until my very heart ached for her.

I thought I knew the whole of her troubles, but I was soon to be terribly enlightened. The week-end before Emmy's first examination was a weary time. The poor child was ill—very ill. "Those ages," "those ages," "those ages," were upon her tongue all the time. Again I tried to laugh her out of her insensate anxiety. But all to no purpose; and Emmy went her way on Monday morning about as pitiable an object as I want ever to see again.

When I came home to tea, my hat and jacket were scarcely upon the peg before I heard Emmy's tearful voice calling me in broken tones from our bedroom, and I remember how I flew up the staircase and stood before her in startled inquiry.

"Oh, don't ask me," she sobbed; "don't ask me—don't ask me!"

Of course, I took it that things had gone badly with Faddy, and smoothing the pillow of the bed across which she had thrown herself, and patting her cheek with a forced air of half-remonstrance, half-levity, I ran downstairs and brought up a cup of the tea that was awaiting us.

But things were more serious. All my oft-successful methods of managing her proved futile. Emmy was not to be comforted. I urged her to drink a sip of tea, and tell me all about it. But I urged in vain.

Then there came a rat-tat of the door-knocker below, and Mrs. Jones was creaking up the stairs to say that Miss Ramsay, of Emmy's Girls' School, had come to see Miss Page.

Emmy wouldn't see her under any circumstances —wouldn't see anybody, or do anything—so I went downstairs in a maze as to what had actually happened. And what should I see, of all things under the sun, but Miss Ramsay crying softly in our room! Something serious was afoot, I could see now; and although, up to this, I had been assuming a front of indifference, I began, all at once, to feel a strange anxiety.

"Oh, Jessie, I *am* so sorry! Whatever shall we do? How does the poor thing take it?" Thus Miss Ramsay.

By this time I was getting a trifle desperate in my confusion, and demanded of Miss Ramsay that she should oblige me by explaining what on earth had happened.

"Don't you know! Oh, it's *too* dreadful! Whoever would have thought it of Emmy?"

"Thought *what*? Thought *what*?" I interposed sharply.

"Then she hasn't told you?"

"No," I answered. "All I know is that when I came home from school I found her lying across the bed, where she's now in a passion of tears."

"Well, *I* must tell you although I scarcely like to mention it." And, with elevated eyebrows and a scared face, Miss Ramsay leaned towards me and whispered, "*Falsification of Registers!*"

"What do you mean?" I inquired, as calmly as I could. "What has this to do with Emmy?"

"Falsification of registers! *Eight children over eight years of age altered to seven, and Miss Page admits having done it herself.* Mr. Merrifield told me that the marks of the alteration were as plain as daylight."

"Rubbish! Don't tell me! Emmy may be silly, but she's not so bad as that. Some mistake somewhere."

Less than this I couldn't say, for Emmy's sake; but I had a black fear that what Miss Ramsay had said was only too true. I knew that Emmy was in a terrible state about "those ages," and simply dreaded to meet Faddy; but she never told me anything about having admitted children over eight.

Miss Ramsay had soon smoothed out her agitation and dried her tears, and was on her way to spread the evil news elsewhere.

With a feeling of utter sickness and dejection, I again sought Emmy. She was still sobbing bitterly.

"My dear old girl, don't cry. I know all about it. However could you?——but no, I must not reprove. Don't cry! Don't cry, my pet."

It was a long time before I could get her into a mood to offer a few disjointed words of explanation, and these she only let fall accidentally between the copiousness of her lamentation.

"Oh, Jess, Jess! What shall I do?—what *shall* I do? How shall I tell mother and father of this terrible disgrace I have brought on them? What will they do to me? Oh, I shall drown myself—I shall drown myself!"

This represents the most that I could get out of the wretched girl; but by-and-by I got her into bed, and scribbled a note off to Miss Totts, asking her to excuse my absence from school the next day. I could clearly see that Emmy must not be left at present.

Elsewhere inquiries were going forward. The Board went into the matter, and Faddy, of course, made things out as black for Emmy as possible; and within a month, during which she had not left her bed, and the greater part of which found her in a raging fever, her fate came down from Whitehall.

Her certificate was cancelled for two years for falsification of registers.*

I cannot try to tell you how I broke it to her, or the new frenzy of grief into which she fell. You will bear with me if I simply add that my poor Em was again in the delirium of brain fever, which lasted for over ten weeks. My own anxieties, and the double task of teaching by day and watching over her by night, were severe enough in all truth, but they will scarce bear mentioning beside her troubles. I tried to minimise the effects of her illness in writing home but it was not long before Mrs. Page relieved me at the bedside. And here she learnt, from the girl's wild babbling, the story of her wrong-doing and its punishment.

Emmy went home when the fever had left her, and hung about the old cottage, the shadow of her old self.

Six months later the red earth showed newly upon a flower-decked grave in the corner of the churchyard, under the big yew-tree.

* For two years the teacher whose certificate is cancelled would be prohibited from working in a Government school. Need I say that at the expiration of the sentence, although nominally free once more to seek service, the odds would be heavy against the teacher ever again being appointed to any office?

And Emmy's old College friends talked things over at the Whitsun Reunion, and I was commissioned to see to the erection of a cross of virgin marble, upon which we inscribed the one word written deeply into all our hearts—the one word "Emmy."

Yes, that is a photograph of our loving endeavour to keep Emmy's memory green.

And see, here in this locket is my poor darling's portrait.

There, hold it yourself while you look at it:

FLORRIE SMITH'S CHOICE.

Florrie Smith had chosen.

Many hours of painful introspection had she inflicted upon herself. The situation demanded this naturally, albeit her conclusion had been arrived at —such is womankind—before she began.

Both George Wooderidge and "Maister Wullie" were certainly most presentable young fellows—good-looking, manly, and good-tempered; and it was Florrie Smith's hard fate to be compelled to choose between them.

Had both of them been of Florrie's "station in life" her difficulty would, maybe, have been greater. But with a woman's inevitable touch of Quixotism she leaned from the first to the young school-master.

It is always "Mary, Mary, quite contrary!"

"Maister Wullie," you must know, was son of Mr. Wilson, and Mr. Wilson was the Rector of Thatchamlet. "Maister Wullie," George, and Florrie had learned their A B C's together at the same desk in the village school under old Mrs. Rudge, in the 'Sixties, before School Boards were thought of.

And although, as time went on, their education followed different lines, they remained members of the same village family till well into their teens. Then " Maister Wullie " went up to Oxford, and village minds henceforward dwelt more on the " Maister" than on the " Wullie," even though the old formula survived to the end.

Florrie's path was fittingly humbler. She was apprenticed as pupil-teacher on the same day as George Wooderidge, and stumbled along for five years in the old school, bequeathing upon her pupils, in her untrained pedagogic zeal, an undying hatred for everything connected with the name of learning.

George did the same. But they compared answers after the pupil-teachers' annual examination, and parsed the " Lady of the Lake " together; so life was not altogether unendurable, after all.

Then came the great change—the great enchantment which by-and-by one begins to recognise as the greatest and cruellest of all disenchantments. Florrie took train one January morning for the United Kingdom Church of England Undenominational Training College for Schoolmistresses, at Newage; and a week later George Wooderidge wrote out a splendid label in his best Darnell's style for his well-roped box with the legend: "George Wooderidge, The College, Saltham, Wellingdon, Oxon."

So three years slipped away, until our boys and girls were boys and girls no longer. George and Florrie had sealed their earlier friendship by swearing eternal devotion to each other during the long sleepy summer holiday—sweeter to the Training College student than to anybody else in the world, I think.

Then George went out into the world in real earnest as an assistant under the London School Board, and Florrie came back as mistress of the newly-opened Infants' Department under the newly-established Thatchamlet School Board.

Meanwhile "Maister Wullie" had taken Orders, and had returned to the old village to assist his father in the cure of souls. Which cure of souls included membership of the School Board, of which Mr. Wilson, the elder, was chairman.

So Florrie saw a good deal of her other admirer, and one fine day "Maister Wullie," after struggling through a lesson on the Sermon on the Mount with Miss Smith's "sixes," hung about till playtime; and then—of all things in the world—proposed to the pretty little Infants' Mistress in her school porch—of all places in the world—from which the shadow of the square tower of the church was effectually blotting the yellow glare of the morning's sun.

And Florrie had put him off in a trembling, uncertain way, and mentioned something indefinite about George Wooderidge.

But "Maister Wullie" tried his luck again under what he deemed to be more propitious circumstances, and this time was very definitely and very finally refused, for, as I have already said, Florrie Smith had chosen.

That "Maister Wullie" was annoyed is to put the matter moderately. His attitude thenceforward was that of studied ignorance of the existence of the Infants' Mistress—a course of action which precisely met her wishes in the matter.

How it came about I don't know; but a month or two later Mr. Wilson took Florrie aside, and in the most kindly and fatherly manner imaginable suggested that Florrie had perhaps made a mistake in coming back to her old school directly she left College. Everybody was so familiar with her; a proper and respectful demeanour in the circumstances was out of the question; and so on and so on.

All of which meant that the Chairman of the Board would be glad if she would send in her resignation; she did. Had Florrie been more worldly-wise she could have brought a pretty hornet's nest about Mr. Wilson's ears for his unjustifiable interference. There were plenty of Radicals in the village nowadays, and a strong Dissenting majority on the new Board. But Florrie, good little soul that she was, never gave these matters a thought. From christening upwards she had been taught to look upon Mr. Wilson as something more than human, if not exactly divine. So she sent in her resignation all in proper form, and duly wrote off to George, telling him of the calamity which had befallen her fortunes.

And George by the next post wrote back exactly the sort of letter you can imagine, the beginning of which soothed Florrie greatly; the middle of it made her wonder whether, after all, she ought not to have resisted Mr. Wilson's charitably-tendered suggestion; whilst as for the last three pages they set her heart in a flutter. For they suggested in the most emphatic manner possible that the solution of the problem would be for Florrie and George to get married at once.

Now Florrie was a shrewd little economist—as women go—and she recognised that George's salary plus Night School work came to exactly fifty shillings a week, with which sum she did not quite see her way to make ends meet at London prices. The less so since George, as she knew, could not have put by much as yet wherewith to start their little household. And for the moment Florrie allowed the dim outline of a parallel to linger in her mind—a parallel which, curiously enough, only strengthened this very sagacious economist in her devotion to George.

However, the end of it was that the Infants' Mistress at Thatchamlet married the Assistant Master at the Urchin Alley Board School, Camberwell, a notice to this effect duly appearing in the columns of *The Schoolmaster*, and I am sorry to say that Florrie mortally offended most of her friends, and seriously annoyed the rest, by absolutely refusing to stand side by side with George at the altar rails of the old church they had attended since children.

Nor could anyone glean the reason except, perhaps, Mr. Wilson senior, who supposed airily, when some village weevil broached the matter to him, that nothing would suit young people nowadays but that they should fling off to London and get married at a Registrar's Office; which wasn't altogether charitable of the Rector under the circumstances, was it?

Six months in a couple of human rabbit-hutches styled by a pretty conceit "Sitting and Bedroom Apartments" off the Camberwell New Road; a course of thoroughly-exhausted London air; long, weary, dead-wall hours of existence for Florrie; and rush, worry, indigestion, and School Board laryngitis for George, had taken the gilt from off the ginger-bread for our young friends.

To pay their way and buy suitable food just about absorbed their monthly wage. The outlook was more than gloomy. Sydney Bale, who had been a pupil-teacher at Thatchamlet ten years before Florrie and George — Sydney Bale, whose renown as a student still lives in the little old-time village — was toiling on in the tenth year of his assistantship under the London School Board, with not the faintest chance of promotion, at a maximum salary, all told, of fifty-four and sixpence a week. Mrs. Bale was a wan-looking, faded little woman who struggled heroically to husband carefully her slender resources and keep a family of six little Bales with their elbows covered and their feet above water. Now and again she added a few pounds to the family exchequer by going "on supply" for a month or so, the net result of which left the family distinctly worse off than before — such is the eternal inexorableness of things domestic.

A contemplation of Bale's career and those of many equally fine fellows in London, and more than one wistful gaze at Florrie's blanched cheeks and brightened eyes, set George a-thinking, with the result that he commenced buying his "Organ" on his way home of a Friday afternoon, and had the first three or four pages ticked off here and there in blue before the little lodgings off the Camberwell New Road were reached.

I do not think the literary contents excited his interest much, and even strenuous advocacy of the "£175 maximum for assistant masters" he threw aside with a heavy sigh.

In all, I think George replied to between eighty and a hundred advertisements. In the beginning he pitched his desires high—even tried for a Higher Grade school at Factory Field. But he came down by a very rapid declension to

> "Country School. Average attendance 120. No Sunday duties. Wife to help with Needlework. Salary inclusive £50 and one-half of Grants received, with a house."

For George had determined to get back again out of stifling, poisoning London, to the countryside, the open moorland, the gorse, and the brake-ferns. There was something in the charm of being a headmaster— even of a country school; and Florrie's health demanded the change. Besides, Florrie could help with the Sewing; and perhaps he might get a private pupil or so; and what with one thing and another, and the relief of being away from the rush and turmoil of London life and lodgings, and the London Chatham and Dover Railway four times a day, why, "they absolutely wouldn't know themselves" settled in a nice flower-clad country schoolhouse!

Six times George was amongst the "selected" candidates, and six times he went back to Camberwell a thoroughly disheartened, broken-down old man of six-and-twenty.

For a time he actually gave up applying, and struggled on with his class of seventy in the malodorous little class-room under the shadow of the South London leather-works. When he wasn't at the Night School, he had to hurry off to a Centre at Battersea to further qualify himself to give "physical instruction." He was the best high jump and half-mile sprinter for six villages around as a young man at home, but that didn't count; he wasn't branded "L. S. B.," so he had to waste weeks doing finnicking hops and twists and going through a variety of pretty movements like an animated chess pawn smitten badly with St. Vitus' Dance.

Then there was the paper-snipping class with advanced students—some of them gray-headed graduates in honours at the London University—

E

whittling away bits of wood at the newly-erected shrine of the great modern Manual Training fetish.

But by-and-by he got his "parchment," and new lodgings had to be taken, for a little Florrie had made her appearance, and George once more bent his back to the task of getting away to the country at all costs. Again the weary, heart-sickening filling-in of Application Forms; and again the copying-out of testimonials, in the terms of which by this time George was absolutely letter-perfect.

One day, some months later, came a letter from the Corresponding Manager of the Little Mosslingham Church of England Schools. The worthy gentleman had read George's application with pleasure, and would like to see him respecting the appointment. Could George come down and meet him at the Marborough Railway Arms Hotel on Saturday at noon—Marborough being the junction for the Little Mosslingham Road Station.

George could and did; and the Rev. Mr. Chittleworth proved so exceptionally amiable, and gave such a glowing account of the desirability of service in the Little Mosslingham School, that George there and then signed an Agreement to commence duties at Lady Day; the said Septimus St. Clair Chittleworth, Clerk in Holy Orders, undertaking on his part and in his capacity as Corresponding Manager for the said Church of England School for Little Mosslingham to pay the aforesaid George Wooderidge, certificated master, the sum of fifteen pounds quarterly, together with, when received, an annual payment of one-half the Government Grant. In consideration of which the aforesaid George Wooderidge on his part and in his capacity as certificated teacher in charge of the said, &c. &c., would conduct the school in accordance with the provisions of the Government Code of Education for the time being as endorsed by the aforesaid and many times previously specified Corresponding Manager, making provision also on his, the aforesaid George Wooderidge's, &c. &c., part, for the teaching of the Needlework.

So George went home, for the first time for many a long day, whistling; and there was great rejoicing that night in the house—or Furnished Apartments rather—of Wooderidge.

For weeks there were great preparations, and the faithful little wife of three years' standing spent her days thereafter in the exhausting and exhilarating— if the conflict of terms may be permitted—work of furniture-hunting.

Easter week found the new schoolmaster, his wife, " Little Flo," and their household gods, most of them newly acquired, deposited upon the single platform of the Little Mosslingham Road Station.

It was raining heavily, unfortunately, and there was a seven miles' ride in a lumbering great four-wheeled waggon George had previously chartered as the most effective conveyance for his purpose.

But the rain was a trifle. The air was such a tonic as only weary, half-asphyxiated town-folk who penetrate right into the heart of the real country can appreciate, and the hedges were spangled with primroses. Much to the amusement of the half-obfuscated waggoner, George insisted upon crying a halt more than once in the pelting rain in order to dash off to some secluded meadow-corner, where the water swished up with every step he took, in order to capture handsful of more than usually glorious Lenten lilies.

But the journey was at an end at last, and Little Mosslingham, straggling around three sides of a great healthy-looking village green, came in view as they breasted the crown of the last hill.

Yes, there was the square-towered church, and a little below it — God's Acre between — the village school, high gabled and roughly hewn, picturesquely garnished by the bright new green of the trees. At its further end the goal of their great desire, the little

School House that was for the future—perhaps until each was old and grey—to be their home; and Florrie breathed a deep prayer of thankfulness as the great waggon lumbered around the green, and the cheap window-blinds of every cottage were drawn stealthily aside, and the bare-footed, soft-eyed youngsters came with a rush to the baby-boards in each open doorway to see the new Schoolmaster arrive.

Now, if George Wooderidge had taken the interest he ought to have done in professional matters, he would not have closed with the Rev. Mr. Chittleworth quite so quickly. If he had studied the experience of others placed under his nose almost weekly, there are several things upon which he would have required enlightenment before burning his boats so completely.

Mr. Chittleworth's description of the School House, for instance, would scarcely have been endorsed by anybody who had had the misfortune to have lived in it. It was not exactly what you would call either a large or a desirable residence. In point of fact, it was a diminutive four-roomed cottage. In its front room downstairs you dared not put a fire for fear of being suffocated, whilst the back room balanced a fire that burnt all right, by a stone floor.

Its south wall was hopelessly soaked with moisture for three-fourths of the year, what wall-paper had retained its adherent qualities displaying quite a botanical museum in the way of rare fungus growths. The outlook at the front was charming; but you leant over the low rough wall along the tiny back-yard to gaze upon the primitive tombs of the departed Mosslinghamites — not an altogether exhilarating prospect at the end of a heavy day's work.

And then the drains! But as apparently there *were* no drains at Little Mosslingham, it would ill become the humbly-stationed schoolmaster to be fastidious.

Easter week had not closed over George and his wife before they very decidedly bated their good opinion of the School House, based upon the Rector's description and a contemplation of its picturesque exterior.

But Monday morning brought the re-opening of the school under the new master, and all were agog for the momentous occasion. Nothing could have exceeded Mr. Chittleworth's amiability. He called at the School House the day after George's arrival, and inquired kindly as to how they were progressing. Could anything be sent from the Rectory for them? So kind was he that George and Florrie agreed that they could not in common decency begin complaining yet awhile. Then Mr. Chittleworth came up to the school on the opening morning, and introduced George to Miss Coles, the Ex-P.T., and Harry Bushell and "M'ria," the pupil-teachers. Also to the children.

"Of course," added the rector, anticipating George, "you won't expect to find everything here brand-new and up-to-date, like you have it in London. We've got to make shift for a good many things in a country school like this. We've the work of the world to get funds enough to keep our heads above water."

This likewise was far from exhilarating, and that night George summed up the situation.

"Well, Flo, this is what I make of it. There are 180 on the books, including infants; the average for last year was 135. Miss Coles takes the infants; Maria Potts Standard I.; Harry Bushell Standard II.; leaving me something like 60 in Standards III., IV. and V., including two girls and a boy in the Sixth—you, of course, helping on Wednesday afternoons with the sewing."

"But, George," interrupted Mrs. Wooderidge, "surely you haven't got to take the four standards alone? And so many of them!"

"So far as I can see, yes," replied George. "The worst of the thing is, they seem to be so badly supplied with material. The desks are a long way worse than anything we ever had at Thatchamlet, and how Barrow passes the Readers I don't know. I feel sorry now I didn't ask Chittleworth something about why Jones left. The log-book is full of complaints written by Jones about the insufficiency of the staff, and the difficulty there has been in getting material. Barrow mentions the poorness of the staff in the last Report, which is a shocking one. If Jones got the sack for it, I should say he wasn't entirely to be blamed by a long way. However, don't let's be despondent about things. Chittleworth seems a very decent sort of chap, and, after all, I should have blown my brains out if I'd stayed at Urchin Alley much longer. And not only that; it *is* a relief to know that I can please myself what I do on Sundays. Chittleworth never mentioned Sunday work when I saw him at the Junction."

And so, as they put out the candle, ended the first chapter of George Wooderidge's Headmastership of the Church of England School at Little Mosslingham.

That George Wooderidge found his work in the school brutally hard, scarce needs the telling. He had sole charge of Standards III., IV., and V., each fairly large, with an odd girl or two and sometimes a boy in the Sixth. He was dodging from standard to standard the whole day long, trying meanwhile to keep an eye on Harry Bushell and

"M'ria," who sorely needed direction at every step they took. Miss Coles he was compelled to leave to her own devices, hopeful at first that a grown-up young woman who had passed the Scholarship would be able to manage the infants without much help from him.

Here, I am sorry to say, his confidence was egregiously misplaced. Miss Coles was easily the most inefficient of his three helpers. Poor girl, she did her best, and strove loyally from morning till night. But she had dropped into teaching, like many another village girl, simply because she was the first individual to hand. She did not profess to have the slightest love for or initiative in her work. Her apprenticeship had been stumbled through, and after twice sitting she had scored a very bad second at the Scholarship. And here she was, George Wooderidge's right-hand man, so to speak, at the princely salary of £25 a year.

Before long, Mrs. Wooderidge's "Wednesday afternoons" came twice and thrice a week, and for three months before the Examination she was in the school almost as many hours a week as her husband.

But here they were: they had got their wish, and spent nearly their last penny in achieving it. Besides, "Number Two" was shortly "expected," and, therefore, if the rector of the parish had asked George to black his boots for him, I don't see how George would have had any alternative but to agree.

And this brings one to another matter upon which George Wooderidge should have asked a question or two before finally committing himself irrevocably to Mosslingham village—it is so provokingly easy to be wise after the event, isn't it? Mr. Chittleworth had described himself all through as the "Corresponding Manager," thereby suggesting by implication that there were *other* managers. Amongst the many revelations George and his wife received during the first week or two of their life at Mosslingham was the fact that Mr. Chittleworth was the Corresponding and *only* Manager, two of his servants signing Form IX.* with him as a pure piece of formality.

The fact that he was completely in the hollow of one man's palm was somewhat disquieting to George; but it was a circumstance, like a good many others, that had to be grinned at and borne.

However, Mr. Chittleworth continued most amiable; and although the work was heavy and luxuries

---

* Form IX. is the Government Return showing an account for the year of all expenditures of money, etc. It must be signed by three persons ostensibly Managers of the School.

were few, the lanes were charming to minds surfeited with the roar and turmoil of South London, milk was fresh, and the countryside broad and open.

George and Florrie were regular in their devotions at the village church, of course, and took their places on Sunday afternoon in the schoolroom, with its ancient desks now rearranged after the method favoured for Sunday-school purposes. But this interest in the spiritual well-being of the village was entirely spontaneous so far as the schoolmaster and his wife were concerned; for apparently Mr. De Muir, the curate to whom Mr. Chittleworth treated himself, acted as superintendent of the Sunday-school.

At any rate, he did for the first three or four weeks; and then one Friday afternoon Mr. Chittleworth came into the school a trifle more amiable even than usual. —"Delighted to find Mr. and Mrs. Wooderidge took such interest in parish affairs."—"Yes, nice little Gregorian service they had got up in the church, wasn't it?"—"Yes, grand old oak screen, wasn't it?" —"Thought it would have been better left unpainted and gilded, eh? Well, yes, perhaps so, perhaps so; matter of opinion, after all, wasn't it?"—"So glad Mr. Wooderidge had such a fine bass voice."—"Yes, sweet-toned little organ, wasn't it?"—"Yes, it *was* a great advantage to have a two-manual."—"Ah, Mr.

Wooderidge had noticed, too, how sweet some of the stops on the great organ sounded."—"That, in *his* opinion, was the feature of the organ."—" Miss Fanny, on the other hand, favoured the swell—like most organists, he supposed."—" Perhaps Mr. Wooderidge would like an occasional practice? If so, the instrument was entirely at his disposal."—"And oh! by-the-bye, *could* Mr. Wooderidge take over De Muir's superintendentship of the Sunday-school for a week or so, and let De Muir get away for a rest?"

" Oh, yes," George would oblige gladly. So Sunday morning saw him installed temporarily as superintendent of the Sunday-school. De Muir was away for a month; and when he came back, such wonders had been worked in the discipline of the Sunday-school that Mr. Chittleworth could not find it in his heart to ask De Muir to resume his duties.

You will probably think George Wooderidge a fool, and tell me he had no spirit; for he allowed himself to be wheedled into taking complete charge of the Sunday-school without a word; being in the full possession of his faculties at the time, and keenly feeling that he *was* being wheedled. But George had not yet received his first quarter's fifteen pounds, which was potent argument number one; and Mrs. Wooderidge's condition gave him some little anxiety, which was potent argument number two. Their little purse was alarmingly low, and, in a word, George was most effectually tied by the leg.

You strident N.U.T.-ists, you Gales and Crofts and Waddingtons and Jackmans!—you, I know, will turn up your high-souled and combative noses in fine contempt of this poor weakling. But let *me* tell *you* that it is no good preaching heroics to a man with an almost empty purse and a sick wife. Let *me* tell *you,* too, that many a fine man has gone the way of George Wooderidge, and has suffered all sorts of tyranny with never a word of revolt—for the sake of the others.

So things went on. Work, hard and engrossing, was the staple of George's life. Quarter-day came round, and happily Mr. Chittleworth paid up promptly. What would have happened if, on this occasion, he had acted as he did many times subsequently, and delayed payment for weeks and even months, I do not like to contemplate.

The worst, however, did *not* happen, and George and his wife felt themselves getting quite nice and straight by the time that "Number Two" arrived, once again to dislocate arrangements and upset calculations, especially those connected with the transactions of the family purse.

Still, the Chittleworths were exceptionally kind. Indeed, Mr. Chittleworth was the most amiable soul under the sun. It was almost impossible to quarrel with him. I think he owed his habitual serenity of mind and geniality of manner to the combination of two abnormally-developed characteristics. He combined the most lively and very real consideration for himself with an utter absence of real consideration for others. It would have nearly killed him if anybody had suggested anything so unchristian and selfish to him; but the fact remained, all the same. His own working powers he knew to be very effectually limited, and those limits he took particular care never to come near reaching. As for all others who came into contact with him, he never seemed to give a thought as to whether *their* endurance might be limited or not. So long as you could bring and carry, the Rev. Septimus St. Clair Chittleworth would find occupation for you. It was always "all hands to the pumps" with Mr. Chittleworth, and nobody could beat him at the work of looking smilingly on.

Mind you, if you were ill, or complained of fatigue, he would gush with a genuine, if momentary, flow of sympathy. But it wouldn't for a moment enter his mind to take your place at the grindstone; and five minutes later he would be laying out plans, with the most childlike enthusiasm, whereby new tasks would fall upon you!

In fact, George Wooderidge very soon found himself doing all sorts of odd jobs out of school-hours without in the faintest degree realising how or when they came upon him, or being able to distinguish between the finely-shaded-off boundary that in this particular case divided Voluntaryism from Compulsion.

At George's first examination Mr. Barrow spoke most hopefully of the splendid foundation he had made, complained in the Report of the inadequate assistance provided, and put our usually placid Mr. Chittleworth into a state of most unwarranted perturbation by demanding before next year something in the shape of a system of drainage for the school, a cloak-room, and a new window for the south wall. Mr. Acland was in office at Whitehall, and Mr. Barrow, wise man that he was, regulated his action accordingly.

Poor Mr. Chittleworth was at his wits' ends. His income was at the very least £700 a year, but then he kept up an expensive establishment, and had a fashionable wife and two fashionable daughters. Beyond his annual subscription of a five-pound note to the funds of the school it never entered his simple mind to dip deeper into his pocket. Besides, look what he gave the school in the way of gratuitous service!

So they got to work beating up for subscriptions, which came in badly. Consider the state of agriculture! Then they gave a concert, for which George and his wife slaved untiringly. The fashionable Misses Chittleworth sang and played little fripperies. Mr. De Muir read a piece—a very long and wearying piece—and the schoolboys found it terribly slow work sitting at the back of the room and clapping for the honour of the village. George sang a couple of bass songs in a way that deserved a bigger and more critical audience. Dr. Brown contributed the comic element; and the Rector filled in the interval with a very earnest little speech, showing what a terrible infliction it would be both upon their consciences as well as their pockets if the dear old school should have to be given up and a detestable School Board take its place.

And what part did Florrie play? A very important and tiring part, I can assure you. Her little household—at any rate, the better parts of it—was given up to the entertainers; and she brewed much tea and coffee and cut up much cake for their delectation. It is surprising what demands such a function makes on the wife of the village schoolmaster, even though she never appears in the Votes of Thanks.

But it was all unavailing; for when the work had been accomplished Mr. Chittleworth found himself £40 to the bad, and when the accounts were squared up he sent for George to see him at the rectory. With an urbanity and amiability beyond all admiration, he unfolded the situation to the much-worried master, and then, after much circumlocution, detailed his plan. It pained him to the quick to have to suggest it; but there was no alternative. He had racked his brain for nights together to find some better means; but all to no purpose; and in the end he had been driven to the only conclusion open to him, and that was to offer George ten pounds a quarter fixed salary instead of fifteen. Of course, George's work merited a much higher remuneration, he knew, and if they couldn't keep him, why, of course they must advertise again, and at the lower figure. He need not say how grievously it had pained him, etc.

George went home to think it over, and realised—Florrie dissenting, curiously enough—that there was nothing for him to do but to accept the reduction. Which he did, squaring matters three months later, when Louisa Coles got married, by adding his wife permanently to the school staff at a salary of £20, Chittleworth assenting. "Little Flo" was now in the Infants' class, and "Number Two," otherwise "George Smith Wooderidge," fared as best he could in the daily care of one Jane Court, widow of a lately deceased labourer.

So far, George had kept clear of the organ, though he sang in the choir, leaving his Sunday-school in the care of old Marks directly he had marched them into their corner in the little aisle. Miss Fanny took the organ and trained the choir. The services were more attuned to Miss Fanny's ideas than the musical education of the villagers, but that was a trifle.

But the organ and choir-training came upon him after the manner of the Sunday-school. Miss Fanny sadly needed a change—poor girl, she did indeed. Mr. Chittleworth would send her up to her cousins in London for a few weeks if it were not for the organ. Ah! happy thought! *Would* Mr. Wooderidge so far place them under an eternal obligation by taking her place for a Sunday or so?

Well, the little Wooderidges had just been down with the measles, during which time nothing could have been kinder than the solicitude of the Chittleworths. If the youngsters had devoured all the preserves sent them from the Rectory pantry something far worse than measles would have befallen them.

So George took Miss Fanny's place after making a very pointed and emphatic reference to the mutual understanding between all parties that his occupancy of the stool was merely temporary. And in due season Miss Fanny returned and resumed control of the musical part of the little church's services. But Fanny's holidays multiplied apace and grew in duration. Besides, George favoured a more simple and congregational form, whilst Miss Fanny revelled in the higher art; and this fact led to interminable little difficulties, which were ultimately solved two years later by George, who was genuinely and enthusiastically fond of music, finding himself one fine day in complete and undisturbed possession of the musical department at Little Mosslingham Church, and by a fine touch of irony his first great success was the brilliant way he made his instrument sing out in a great pæan of joy Mendelssohn's "Wedding March" on the occasion of Miss Fanny's wedding.

And so the years went on, and George was getting grey above the ears and prematurely lined about his eyes. Florrie had settled down into a hard-working, pale-featured, all-encompassing little woman-of-all-work. What George would have done without her

I do not pretend to suggest. Their little covey of hopefuls now numbered five, and though each new addition fettered the shackles upon George's independence more securely and tightly than before, yet, on the whole, Florrie and he many times agreed that, after all, life at Little Mosslingham would be unendurable without them.

And so, I repeat, by way of filling in in a phrase a big slice of existence, the years slipped on. George had given the best years of his life to Little Mosslingham. There was absolutely no hope of professional advancement before him. Indeed, he didn't look for *that*, so convinced was he of its utter unattainability. He continued to drudge along with inefficient help in the school, Florrie's untiring devotion notwithstanding. And as a matter of fact his average salary, after all these years of faithful service, was smaller than his first year's return at Mosslingham by between twenty and twenty-five pounds.

He was now one of the standing institutions of the village, and could scarcely call a waking hour his own from dawn on Sunday to dark on Saturday night. It was "Mr. Wooderidge this" and "Mr. Wooderidge that" at every turn. Sunday-school, choir, organ, cottage flower show, and I know not what else. Nevertheless he was as contented as a village schoolmaster may fairly hope to be under existing conditions—and in this world.

Occasionally he pondered over what was to become of him and the wife when brain and hand gave out, "and all the weary wheels stand still."

And, by-the-bye, what *does* become of our worn-out village schoolmasters? Several hundreds are basking their declining years in the sun of a nation's gratitude with little pensions of twenty, twenty-five, and thirty pounds a year, I know, and many of course die in harness, hanging on in their office until the last pulse, through dire necessity. Several within my knowledge are to-day in the Workhouse — fitting close to lives of drudgery in the nation's interest. They couldn't die before dismissal came, or I think they gladly would have done. Bah! Let us leave the subject: it makes one's fingers itch to get up and shake somebody or other into an appreciation of the country's duty in the matter.

Occasionally, I say, George Wooderidge pondered gloomily over the future. Its brightest possibility was that he should work on undisturbed at Little Mosslingham as long as his energies permitted, and then become the pensioner of his children. "Little Flo" was now at Redlands in her Second Year, and she would be off their hands soon. George and his wife had vowed many a time never to make a child of theirs a teacher, but help was sorely needed in the school, and nobody could be secured, and Flo seemed so apt and resourceful before a class that she dropped naturally into her indentures, just as naturally as did young George, who had just passed his Second Year's Pupil Teachers' Examination with flying colours. Probably the younger members would follow suit in time.

Harry Bushell, Wooderidge's first Pupil-Teacher, was now a B.Sc. of London, and Director of the Polytechnic in Great Queen Street, earning a salary that made his old master's mouth water. Yet he contemplated the good fortune of many of his old pupils with heartfelt pride, and contrasted their careers with his own with scarce a twinge of envy.

Everything seemed to point to George's ending his professional days at Little Mosslingham, when an event occurred that revolutionised the steady course of affairs. That event was no more and no less than the passing of the Local Government Act, and the conferring on Little Mosslingham of the unlooked-for benefaction of a Parish Council.

Now, Mr. Chittleworth was an old-world feudal politician of the most beneficent and charitable type, and nothing more hugely amused him in all his existence than this gift from the gods of a Parish Council for his little village. Look at it seriously he would not; its contemplation in that light hurt his dignity. Was he not Parish Council enough for Mosslingham?

But the Parish Council came, and rightfully or wrongfully Mr. George Wooderidge—at his time of life, too—must needs take a lively interest in its fortunes.

Yes, he would stand as a Councillor, and, if a poll were demanded, would certainly go through with the thing.

All of which he did, to Mr. Chittleworth's unspeakable disgust.

During the preliminaries George and his "Corresponding Manager" had more than one wordy tussle, and, when a poll found the village schoolmaster's name at the top, Mr. Chittleworth declared war in earnest, and told his schoolmaster flatly that one thing or the other must be given up—the school or the Parish Council.

And will it be believed that, after all the pliability he had shown, and after sacrificing principles right and left for years in order, as I take it, that he might be "agreeable-like," George Wooderidge was mad enough over this paltry Parish Council business to get his back up and defy Mr. Chittleworth to do his worst?

I'm not sure that, when he came calmly to face

the future, immediate and prospective, he didn't wish the Local Government Act and its Parish Council a thousand miles under the sea. But the die was cast, and climb down he would not, argue as much as they liked. So there was for the moment much weeping in the little Schoolhouse, and then a brave-set little heart got to work once more to face the terrors of an unknown future. And the three months' notice was received with outward equanimity, even though father and mother felt unknown dread as they glanced around their little household.

Three months!—three months in which to tear up old, deeply-imbedded roots, to sever almost life-long connections, and to find a new home! And George on the wrong side of forty!

Ah! then he knew the bitterness that falls on the elementary schoolmaster who seeks a new post after his fortieth birthday has been reached. It is not ripe, wise, fatherly, beneficent influence that is needed in our schools. Certainly not. What is wanted is rapid, slap-dash, up-to-date methods of negotiating big Government Grants on the precocious achievements of the pupils.

So the three months slipped by as three days, and George Wooderidge was no nearer a new post than when he started.

But it was a brave-set little face that went down the hill by his side in the great lumbering waggon—a face that flinched only once; and that was when a big tear splashed heavily on the hard-wrought little hand that was trying its hardest to carry comfort and support in the clasp in which it held the fingers of the beaten and dejected man, into whose face a new sear had worked its way, into whose heart a new hardness.

It was a brave little face that gave way to a torrent of tears as the train jolted out of the Mosslingham Road station—a brave little face that had the crying children reflecting its own smiles before the first station four miles down the line had been reached.

At Marborough George had taken lodgings; he could not face Thatchamlet, even though most of his old acquaintances had forgotten him. For three months he wrote and posted morning, noon, and night. From the first the family put the most rigid limit upon their expenditure in the only two necessities they dared purchase—lodgings and food.

The girls at Redlands wondered why Florrie Smith, one of the happiest of their number, became suddenly so worried and anxious about something or other. They wondered that, as the year wore on and winter approached, she didn't go out with the other girls for the usual walks. So did Miss Mellish, the matron. And, indeed, I know Florrie had to make some confessions to her which gave them mutual pain for the moment—confessions which led to a delicately tendered act of generosity on Miss Mellish's part, which Florrie was by no means such a prig as to reject. Whatever the incident was—I have never pressed for the details—it has made Florrie and Miss Mellish friends for life; and as for Florrie—well, Miss Mellish is her particular heroine. I happen to know that one of Florrie's earliest purchases after she had left College, and the family had got straight again, was a grand fur-lined cloak for Miss Mellish, which was a curious gift under the circumstances, wasn't it?

Down at Marborough the cloud looked heavy indeed. Wooderidge not only applied for every school, likely or unlikely, that presented itself, but he scoured the local and country papers at the reading-rooms for situations of any sort that seemed to offer him a chance, and always with one heart-sickening result.

He had been disheartened with his want of success in the old time, when, as a London assistant, he had tried to get down into a country school. But what would he not have given to have exchanged his chances to-day with those of that self-same assistant. And this after many years' experience and meritorious service in the very class of school in which he was seeking employment!

Christmas was nearly upon them, and with it desperation. I cannot follow them through all their suffering. It is a thing about which I, at any rate, prefer not to speak. But at last, when the thread of endurance seemed on the point of wearing through, fortune smiled.

Mrs. Wooderidge says she recognised the writing at once, but that was surely an after-thought.

At any rate, here is the letter: Mr. Wooderidge has extracted it for the moment from the sacred contents of his locked drawer in order that I might copy it:—

"THE RECTORY, MONKHAMPTON,
"*2nd February*, 189—.

"MY DEAR WOODERIDGE,—I am delighted and surprised to find you are a candidate for the Headmastership of our school. Thatchamlet and my father's testimonial — your earliest—caught my eye directly I opened your application. I have wondered many a time what had become of you and your wife. I remember Florrie, as if it were yesterday, through all these years. Since I left Thatchamlet and took this living, I have seemed to lose sight of all the old folk.

"If you think this little school good enough for you, and are willing to accept the terms, the post is yours. The present master has been here over forty years, and is now retiring on a Government pension I've managed to secure for him. I am afraid for a long time past he hasn't been up to Worrier's idea of what is essential for young Giles's future, and our grants have suffered. In fact, Worrier hinted very plainly to me several examinations ago that the school would never be what it should be until Sampson was cleared out. But I gave him such a warm quarter of an hour as he has rarely experienced, so he has never broached the topic again. And as for Sampson, he might have stayed on till he was stone-deaf before *I* would have suggested his retirement. He is now teaching the second generation here, and is held in about ten times the reverence I am — naturally, I being a comparatively newcomer. It was only at the old man's express wish that I set about getting him this paltry Government pension, which, by the way, we shall supplement by £20 a year and a cottage.

"So, my dear George, the place is yours for the asking. It is a very nice little school, with eighty on books. There is an endowment from the Rowe Charity of sixty pounds a year, to which the Governors—who are, as a matter of fact, very much sleeping partners in the concern so long as all goes well—have added another forty to make up the master's salary. The school is excellently furnished, and we reckon to keep things—exclusive of master's salary and residence—going on the grants, which I don't think you will find a hard job. What do you say? Now that Sampson is leaving, we shall build a new schoolhouse for the master, as the old one is a trifle small. Can you come down and see me? Write by return. My kind regards and remembrances to Mrs. Wooderidge and yourself. What family? We have six torments, big and little, to make life endurable.—Believe me, Very sincerely Yours,

"W. W. WILSON.

"P.S.—I see you can get through from Marborough Junction to Fairfax Gate, our nearest station, by a train that leaves

Marborough at 8.37 in the morning. You will have an hour and a half to wait at Streetley, getting to Fairfax Gate at 3.58, when I will meet you with the dog-cart if you write. We can put you up for the night, and you can return the next day."

I had a mind to leave my story here, because there is really nothing more to tell. George jumped at the really splendid and unique opportunity opened out to him through the influence of old times and almost forgotten associations, and Monkhampton turned out all that "Maister Wullie" had painted it, and more.

There is little or nothing of the parson and the schoolmaster between the Wilsons and the Wooderidges. The families fraternise in the most complete manner. Mrs. Wilson thinks little Mrs. Wooderidge the best little wife any schoolmaster under the sun could possibly possess; and Mr. Wilson heartily agrees. "Young Flo," or "*née* Miss Florence Smith Wooderidge, L.L.A.," as I had better style her, is home for the Christmas holidays, and "Young George," who—notwithstanding that he lost a year of his apprenticeship—came out fifth in the Scholarship List last midsummer, has been three months at the old college at "Saltham, Oxon."

"Little Flo," I regret to have to say, has only just escaped a fine of seventy pounds, I think the sum is, for not having taught in a Government school until the receipt of her parchment. For last Monday week, being popularly known as "Boxing Day," she relinquished school work for ever, I hope, and took instead the heart and arm of your very obedient, the narrator of this faithful history.

And the "Wedding March," they tell me—for I cannot recall a note of it—pealed out in a way that Monkhampton never dreamed of before, though it was *not* George Wooderidge who was at the organ.

And there were tears of gladness from full hearts at the altar-rails; and a brave little face was lit up with a smile of great peace of mind and happiness. Nor was there one thought of flinching in that brave little face as a great tear splashed heavily on the four big brown fingers trying their hardest to carry comfort and support in the clasp in which they held a hard-wrought little hand—the hard-wrought little hand of the woman who five-and-twenty years since had chosen, chosen with a choice in which she has rejoiced through storm to sunshine, through crushing sorrow to sweet and lasting peace.

BY ORDER OF THE BOARD.

"HERE's your class, Mr. Ashford, and I've no doubt you'll get on all right!"

Mills, the headmaster, turned carelessly away; the scientific little snick of the door sent just the suspicion of a flutter of nervousness into Charlie Ashford's heart, and he was alone with the eighty little urchins henceforward to be his charge at the Wharf Back Board School, Shadford.

Charlie was a fine sample of the clean-limbed, high-purposed young fellows sent out year by year from the Training Colleges to have their souls crushed out of them in the great School Board mill.

Charlie had read widely outside his College text-books, and had found teaching most congenial to his generous and sympathetic nature in the exhortations on behalf of the workers by the Socialist and Fabian essayists. He rejoiced that it should have been given him to go down into the dark places of Shadford. He, too, would take his share in the fight against ignorance and destitution. His boys should be raised out of the grim pit in which Chance had decreed that they should be born. Their heads should be lifted up, their eyes set upon a great ideal, their feet planted upon the firm rock of self-respect and honest endeavour.

And as he stood for the moment all alone in the world, with eighty pairs of diamond-pointed eyes gleaming out at him from under shocks of tousled hair, he felt indeed that his wish had been fully granted, that there would be work here in which in very truth his heart should revel.

But Charlie's flash of thought was rudely switched off in entirely another direction.

Could he believe his ears? The whole class was humming, in a low, fiendish undertone, "And her golden hair was hanging down her back!"

The game had begun. According to invariable custom the young larrikins were going to try conclusions with the new master. Whichever won in this fateful encounter would henceforth rule. If Charlie got the upper hand, he would have, as things go, only an ordinarily hard time in the school as long as he remained in it. If he lost, God help him. For these interesting little studies, pregnant as they were with the possibilities of a great nation's great future, would make his life one long writhe of exquisite torture.

Charlie Ashford was accounted a smart teacher in the Practising School and away down in the little Devonshire village in which he had learned the elements of his art. But two years in the Training College, with only six weeks of actual teaching, had caused him to forget the old knack. So, as his eighty little hopefuls hummed out the hideous refrain, louder and louder as they went on, he gazed from right to left, helpless and distracted.

Perhaps he ought to have fetched Mills, the headmaster; but he had too much of the instinctive pride of the teacher in him to do this.

"Thrash a few," you say? Exactly. Only the School Board, in its wisdom and well-intentioned ignorance of the true bearings of things, went shrieking mad if the lightest finger of correction were laid upon the sacred person of one of these dear little children by anybody save the head teacher.

And even *he* had to act with the most ridiculously painstaking caution. He had to enter what punishment he gave in a book specially provided for the purpose. And it was accounted to him for brutality if the number of his entries exceeded what ought, in the opinion of the dear kind lady who was the visiting member of the Board, to have sufficed under the circumstances.

So Mills, the headmaster, naturally shrank from doing the right thing by these little urchins, though he bitterly knew that many of them would appear hereafter in the criminal dock because of the lack of restraint under which they grew up at school.

Many a time an assistant, at his very wits' end—a grown man, mark you, with children of his own at home—has sent kicking, biting, swearing young riversiders to Mills to be punished, only to have them sent back to the class-room, more contumacious than ever, with a word of warning from the master, who was afraid to punish them.

And then when some young ruffian gets sent to jail for burglary—or to the gallows for worse—good pious people lift their hands in despair and cry, "And this after twenty-five years of Compulsory Education!"

How the gods must laugh at it all in the background!

But I must get back to the Standard III. room and Charlie Ashford and his four-score musicians. Charlie knew that the great struggle had begun. Others who had been through the mill had told him all about it. It was now or never with him. Had he been a free agent, he would have taken a couple of ringleaders and touched them up smartly.

I have stood in Charlie's shoes, so I know.

I remember looking around me—my particular baptism was in the days of "Tommy make room for your uncle" and every boy had his pockets stuffed with stones—for a stick wherewith to coax order. (I knew the regulations, and had taken the oath. But I argued that this was a crisis in which Regulations must go to the wall.)

Behind a cupboard I found a pointer, and I hear ringing in my ears now the shriek of jeering laughter as I took it in my hands and looked vicious. It was hollow and made of thin rolled cardboard; it wouldn't have hurt a fly! The tender-hearted members of the Board had "expected me," as somebody says in *Falka*, and had made arrangements accordingly.

But there was soon a modulation to the minor key on the part of my young heroes. For I remember I put my knee through a big slate, and taking one of the longer frames—well, you can imagine the rest. For the remainder of the day we got on admirably; and if I had stayed years in that school my boys and I would have grown closer friends with every succeeding day. But I didn't stay, and the wherefore of that matter may be set down another day.

Charlie was more conscientious than I was. He would not call Mills; *that* would be *infra dig*. He could not strike a child; *that*, in accepting office, he had pledged himself on no account to do. So he faced the music all the morning until twelve struck at last—years seemed to have elapsed since he found himself shut in alone with his tormentors—and the eighty little gems of the Wharf Back Standard III. went cock-a-hooping down the stairs.

Charlie went round to his lodgings with but little heart for a fried beefsteak. It was touch-and-go that he ever turned up again that afternoon; but there were moneys to be sent home, for the College career had been long and expensive.

When they went into his room at the close of afternoon school they found him picking little red lumps of soft clay off the walls. The drains were "up" outside the schools, and Charlie's beauties had each returned to the fray with a supply of red clay. Walls and windows were peppered with it as the afternoon's torture progressed.

And yet Charlie had kept his temper and his regulations! He mentioned the state of affairs to his fellow-assistants, and they counselled recourse to Mills and cursed the silly rules which encouraged audacious impudence to be even more daring. They had no doubt it would all come right in the end, as it had done, more or less, in their cases. The boys would soon get tired of the pace, and Charlie would get inured; and the two agencies, working together, would in the long run render life a shade or two better than quite intolerable.

Tuesday morning brought Charlie to school with a growing sense of dogged determination. He would *not* lift his finger against a boy; he would *not* call in Mills. He would win them over by steady impregnable patience.

But he had not reckoned on pea-shooters. And the morning's manœuvres included a plentiful display of skill in these instruments of torture.

Charlie shut his teeth as the windows and blackboard rattled, and determined to be patient. But, turning round sharply from the task of writing up some pretty poetry on the blackboard about "The autumn winds are sighing," and various phenomena associated therewith, he received full in the open eye a pea, shot with unusual force by a little rascal in the front row of the desks.

Stinging with the pain, he darted forward and struck the boy a smart blow across the ear with his open hand. The boy dodged adroitly, but failed to escape the blow, which, indeed, helped to send his head with a bang against the iron edge of the desk, inflicting a rather bad cut across the right temple.

There was a howl of pain from the boy, a jerk of horror from the exasperated assistant, the class-room door snicked sharply open, and in rushed a clergyman in the wildest state of gesticulative excitement.

It was the Reverend Isaac Chawley, M.S.B., one of the smuggest humbugs I ever hope again to meet.

Chawley had been indulging his notorious weakness for peering through the windows of the class-room door, noting how things were progressing with the new assistant.

"*You have struck him, sir—you have struck him! I saw you; I saw you—I saw you myself! Oh, look at the blood! look at the blood! My poor child! my poor child!*"

And Chawley's attitude was a thing to be remembered.

Ashford mumbled out something, but Chawley continued—

"*Boy, fetch Mr. Mills here at once!*"

Mr. Mills came, and there were more exhibitions of Chawley's intense solicitude for the poor stricken child, and his more intense execration of the brutal conduct of the assistant. And the end of the matter was that Charlie Ashford was forthwith suspended by Chawley, in his capacity of Chairman of Managers and member of the School Board.

So Charlie went home a desperate man.

Within the week the Managers met, and under Chawley's guidance sent up a crushing resolution to the Board urging Ashford's instant dismissal.

Thereafter the "Teaching" Committee passed judgment on the following Monday, and when Friday came round the S.M.C.* ordered Charlie to appear before it if he had anything to urge in mitigation of the sentence about to be passed upon him.

But Charlie Ashford had nothing to urge in extenuation of his fault, and didn't even turn up at the meeting.

So Chawley, who had been helping to set the town by the ears for six weary hours the previous afternoon at the Board meeting with wire-drawn and noisy disquisitions upon the teaching of Christ's Divinity in the schools, unctuously moved "That the finding of the local Managers and of the 'Teaching' Committee that Mr. C. Ashford, Assistant in the Wharf Back School, be dismissed the service of the Board, be and hereby is endorsed."

* School Management Committee.

Which was done in the twinkling of an eye, *nemine contradicente.*

And I marvel at the fact that one or two of those who are popularly known as the most advanced and enlightened of the Educationists on the Board were, as they usually are, the loudest and the bitterest in their denunciations of the teacher's conduct.

And that night, near the Shadford Road Station, on the West Eastern Railway, they picked up the mangled body of a respectable young man, upon whose remains they held an inquest on the following Monday.

The one solitary gleam of reason and common sense about the whole of the pitiable business was the rider the jury added to their verdict of "Suicide whilst of unsound mind," to the effect that the School Board had acted very harshly in their treatment of the deceased.

But it is somewhat disquieting to know that one or two, at any rate, of the zealous Religionists and the high-souled Educationists at the School Board sneered superciliously when they had recounted to them the comment which had been made upon their conduct by a mere ignorant Coroner's jury.

TRULY RURAL

"WAL'R" HARRIS avoided one terrific mistake to fall into another.

He steadily declined to go under the London School Board as an Assistant: therein he was wise.

Hugh Moss, who passed the Scholarship when Harris was in the First Standard, had been fourteen years under the Board as an Assistant. He began at less than two pounds a week, and he hadn't yet reached the maximum of three. He had, however, acquired a wife and six little Mosses; and, not having the faintest prospect of promotion under the Board, he was about as pitiable an example of a thoroughly disappointed man as you would be likely to meet in a month of days' marches.

Hugh was a First Class man—sixth on the "Borough" List at leaving—and it was the consciousness of the fact that he ought to have done better that made him so bitterly cynical. His headmasters—he had worked with three during his service under the Board—with one voice spoke of him as far and away the most reliable and able colleague it had ever been their good fortune to have with them.

But Moss disdained the petty means by which certain much inferior men to him had gained promotion. For the purposes of "Form 40"* he declined to admit that he "took the liveliest interest in his boys out of school."

As a matter of fact, he had taught many a grimy little London gamin to swim at the Crown Baths on a summer evening; but such contemptible use was made by those keen for advancement of little things like these, that Moss preferred to keep silent about them.

He would not advertise himself as having taken batches of his pupils of a Saturday to the Crystal Palace, the Tower, the Law Courts, and the Houses of Parliament. Neither would he make a great show of the cricket and football clubs he had organised. And as he took no public part in the displays at the Albert Hall, members of the Board, as a rule, were absolutely ignorant of his existence.

When they came into his room he went on as usual—steadily, faithfully, and educationally. He was,

---

* "Form 40": the form of application for appointment and promotion under the London School Board.

of course, courteous and respectful—that goes without saying—but as he was above trotting out showy lessons and posing as a most exceptionally model teacher, members of the Board, good souls! went away thinking what a slow sort of fellow he was, to be sure!

So, on a consideration of these phenomena, "Wal'r," as we used to call him, emphatically declined service under the London Board.

But, as I have already said, he avoided one terrific mistake to fall into another. He thought he saw his way to a steady life, "full of sweet dreams, and health, and quiet breathing," in the bye-ways of Arcadia. So he went down to Chewton Bunney as headmaster of the Board School.

"Wal'r" was a man of the highest purpose, and a teacher by instinct. I wonder life at Chewton didn't break him entirely. Happily, a crisis arose which curtailed his stay there.

Chewton Bunney rejoiced in a School Board of five members—the vicar of the parish, the Rev. Hearty Goodman, three small farmers, and an ex-policeman. I think it was Mr. Goodman's influence that kept "Wal'r's" head above water so long; for the farmers and the ex-policeman would have made even Job's gorge rise.

"Wal'r's" first great disillusion brought home to him the simple fundamental fact that, with the exception of Goodman, not a single member of his Board cared two straws for education.

"Look-a-'ere," said Mugford, the chairman (the vicar was in a Conservative minority of one on the Board), taking "Wal'r" aside the afternoon of his appointment; "wat uz wants yew to du yer, iz to let things go quiet-loike. The mistake yew chaps makes iz tu fancy that schoolin's the on'y thing gwine. Wereaz, it ain't by a long way. A coorse uz wants yew to earn gude grants out a Guvment. That lets uz down easy-loike wi' the rates. A coorse, a coorse. The bigger the Guvment grants yew lays 'old on, the less *we* 'as to pay! Zee? But wat *yu've* got to du iz to get yer Guvment grants and zay nort to nobuddy. That's yer line. Zee? Oi reckons this yer schoolin', a lot uv it, beastly rot. But there 'tis; and we've a got to stand it, Oi spose.

"On'y, the chap wat's now a-going, cum it a bit tu thick. 'E wuz allus a-worritin' on us for this and that. Lor' blessee, life wadun worth livin' vor'n! Oi never cumd inside the blessed door but wat 'e wuz at me about somethin' or other wanted vur the schule. Nothin' wuz gude enough for'n.

"Wy, wan mornin' he complained about the zun

in the middle winders, and ups and axes for sum blin's. Oi ups and Oi zes, quite frenly-loike, 'Alright, Maister Everutt, Oi'll sendee down some Guana-bags.' 'E looks at me 'ard vur a bit, and then he ups and tells me it ain't no jokin' matter! That wuz ees nasty way—grateful for nort. And woodee b'lieve it? 'e ackually 'ad the imperence to tell uz to our fazes that it wuz a disgrace that the schule vloor 'adun' bin scrubbed these vower yers. Ees, Gospel! And Maister Goodman—bah, Oi never cude abide 'e; 'ees nothin' to no place!—Maister Goodman a zaid as 'ow 'e wadun' zo var out!

"But Oi reckons us pit a stapper on *ees* nonzens. He! he! Oi 'ears az 'ow er ab'n got a noo sitiwation yet. He! he! Sarves 'un darn well right, zes Oi!"

And Mr. Chairman Mugford stumped out of the schoolroom door, kicking his "ship-dog" as he went.

A word or two with Everett, the departing master, to whom the Board had granted the privilege of resignation as a clement alternative to three months' notice to quit, endorsed "Wal'r's" view that he had taken on a lively sort of job at Chewton Bunney. But he would need to think once or twice before he went back on his engagement. And as Mr. Goodman took him home to tea, and talked things over in a genuinely helpful sort of fashion, "Wal'r" left the village a trifle assured.

So, to make a long matter short, Walter Harris, anxious to retire to the quiet and seclusion of a country school, became head of the school at Chewton Bunney.

Now, apart from the crushing drudgery of the work—there were six standards to teach, to say nothing of the infants, and Walter's lieutenants were a boy pupil teacher, a monitress, and a makeshift at fifteen pounds a year, technically known as "a woman over eighteen," who, though more than eighteen chronologically, was considerably less than seven intellectually — apart, I say, from the crushing drudgery of the work, apart from the utter absence of any sentiment anywhere in Chewton in favour of education, apart from the lack of sympathy, and apart from the sore need of proper and sufficient apparatus, Walter's greatest obstacle was the irregular way the children attended.

Walter had a big share of common sense, and recognised the presence of many reasons militating against regular attendance at school. Distance from the school, long lanes, dirty weather, the measles, and all the rest of it, were freely written off by him as representing irremovable obstacles to good attendance at school.

But what ate into his soul was the fact that four of the five members of the Board frankly made it a plank in their election platform that their neighbours should on no account be worried about school attendance nonsense. Consequently, Sisyphus's task was, as the vulgar put it, a fool to Walter's. Of course, a certain small section of the children came with the greatest regularity, but with the vast majority it was decidedly a case of "go as you please." Continuity in the instruction was supremely out of the question. To every step forward there were half-a-dozen of marking time for the regular pupils, whilst Walter turned his wits inside out in order to bring the laggards forward under some systematic plan.

In the early days he ventured to remonstrate with Mugford and the other members of the Board; but all to no avail.

What! issue a summons? Why, the heavens would fall! Eh? Grimes, the labourer at Lower Colt's-foot Farm, had three children, *ætat.* seven, nine, and eleven, who had never been to school in their lives and were working about on the farm daily? Well, what o' that? Let 'em work! "*Oi* went out to work at zeben meself"—thus Mugford—"an' look at me *now*—biggest varmer for tain mile roun'. Look at me *now!* Which o' them there buke-larnin' chaps could du ees vowerteen dreepennorths of geen at the 'Cherry Archard' wi' me, and *then* ride the vastest cob in North Rutshire 'ome wi'out turnin' a 'air? Ay! and no parish lantern either!"

Which was simply unanswerable.

So by-and-by Walter gave it up, and ceased expostulating even with Smugley the ex-policeman—Smugley the member of the School Board whose three youngsters attended a shade worse than the worst of them.

Then Walter fought long and doggedly about another matter. It was provided in the Board's Bye-Laws that those children who *did* come to school should not go out to the fields "half-time" until they had passed the Second Standard—"full-time" when the Fourth had been reached.

But the retention of these provisions on the paper containing the Board's Bye-laws was something in the nature of a colossal joke. Nobody took any notice of these qualifying conditions, and there never was a time when each of the three farmer members of the Board was not himself illegally employing boys whose educational equipment was below the meagre standard which the Board nominally set itself to maintain. Walter chafed under this a good deal, begged, prayed, and remonstrated, and then wrung his hands in helpless despair, and gave this up too.

Sneercombe, the Government Inspector, might have helped him vastly. He might have come down smartly on Mugford and the rest of them. Indeed, the law armed him with machinery for declaring the Board in default, and for the election of a new Board by the Education Department at the expense of the locality. *That* would have developed a conscience in Chewton, and no mistake!

But Sneercombe airily waved away any suggestion that he ought, for the children's sake, to move in the matter; and no doubt thought to himself, with a cynical smile, the best way to keep things quiet and comfortable would be to let 'em stew in their own juice. And, so far as Sneercombe was concerned, they stewed.

So, after a couple of years of worrying and badgering, "Wal'r" resolved philosophically to let his Board members alone—which policy readily gained for him their very much enhanced goodwill.

"Wal'r" lodged with Mrs. Crump, a gossipy, kindly old body, who, together with Mr. Goodman, seemed about the only person in the village who entered into the grievous difficulties by which the young schoolmaster was surrounded.

The parents admitted " 'e got the children on nicely "; but they weren't quite sure that it wasn't all a fad; and they insisted upon it amongst themselves that "the schulemaister's" keen desire to see the children regular at school arose from the fact that their attendance meant untold wealth from some source or another to him!

"Oi 'ears as 'ow 'e do earn near on two poun' ten on every one as passes."

"Do er really! No wonder 'e's so sharp on us poor volk about a zending on 'em reg'lar."

This is how the thing presented itself to the average village mind.

Mr. Goodman was Walter's main stand-by. A poor man, he knew the calamity which befalls a clergyman who takes over a village living *minus* a long purse. But what he could do he did, even to the extent of acting—not much to his own advantage, I think—as, in a general way, honorary attendance officer for the school. His visits to Walter's little front-room at Mrs. Crump's were the most welcome events of the week's round, though, indeed, it didn't improve Walter's standing with the other members that Goodman and he should be such excellent friends.

Walter had not been more than a couple of years in Chewton before he felt the work and the worry telling heavily upon him. Then he came to the conclusion that he wanted some change of occupation for his leisure hours, and instead of buying a bicycle he determined to read for the London Matric.

He spent his next winter at this, Goodman helping him generously with knotty bits of Virgil and the tougher tangles of the mathematics. But after a four-winter-months' stretch of the work of the school by day, paraffin oil by night, and the worry of the situation all the while, he was compelled to give up his studies for the time, taking instead, as the spring came on, to long walks.

It was on one of these more or less aimless perambulations that he found himself outside the wall of the big yard in front of Great Barton, Mugford's farm. And who should hail him but Mugford himself? Whatever Mugford's faults may have been, inhospitality was not one of them; and nothing would suit but that the young schoolmaster should step inside and "'ave a drap o' zider," which Polly Mugford brought.

Whether the contemplation of the situation inspired Mugford at the moment, or whether the thing had been fructifying in the worthy chairman's mind for some time, I cannot say, but he had certainly arrived at the conclusion that it wouldn't be half a bad thing for Polly to be married to the agreeable and presentable, if somewhat soft, young schoolmaster.

So Mugford entered quite interestedly into the lonely life it must be for a young chap to be in lodgings, and so on. And before Walter stepped into the highway again he had promised to call in whenever he should be passing that way on his rambles.

Now, Walter was very far from being smitten by Polly Mugford. Polly was a buxom, "slummicky" sort of girl—to use a very expressive term—who had "finished" her education at "boording schule." She was, except when a lazy fit took her, a useful girl about the farm, and had brought home from "boording schule" the art of giving very funny renderings on the wiry piano, with dumpy fat fingers, of "Silvery Waves," "The Maiden's Prayer," "La Châtelaine," and about three other pieces I have forgotten.

But Walter Harris would as soon have thought of enlisting for a soldier as of imagining himself tied for life to Polly Mugford. Indeed, he never thought about the matter at all, and therefore called in at the chairman of the Board's several times during the next month or so: it is such a treat to have somebody to talk to when you are in the country and in lodgings.

Mugford had evidently communicated his ideas to his daughter—the mother had been dead these ten years—and if Harris hadn't been so exceptionally quiet and absorbed a young man *he* would have seen, in Polly's manner at church, that which would have disturbed his equanimity a trifle.

To everybody else it was clear that, upon even this slender warrant, Polly considered the schoolmaster her especial property. And it was because Mr. Goodman saw that something of the sort was in the wind that he ventured lightly to touch upon the subject next time he called in to have a cup of tea with " Wal'r."

His mention of the matter as completely undeceived him as it astonished " Wal'r," who laughed more boisterously than even Mr. Goodman had ever known him to do. But as a result of Goodman's assurance that Polly evidently had her weather eye upon him, Walter's decision was made. He took particular care never to pass Great Barton Farm again in his peregrinations.

This brought Mugford out; and with the rough hand of his type. Without any preamble he plunged into the middle of things after the next monthly committee meeting at the school, and rallied Walter on his negligence! "Miss Polly was getten quite off her feed since Maister 'Arriss 'a ad stopped off a cumin up!"

Now, here was a howde'do for an entirely innocent and rather simple-minded, but very earnest, very honest, and altogether straightforward young man. However, he got out of the difficulty for the time being by the extremely unwise expedient of temporising. He sniggered a bit, and mumbled out a word or two incoherently, and Mugford sheered off, confident that enough had been effected for the present.

Directly Mugford had gone, it dawned upon Walter that he ought to have faced the situation promptly. But second thoughts are often the best.

All he could do was to continue his policy of careful abstention from Mugford's, which, of course, brought Mugford again to the charge. Nor was Polly's by any means a secret, silent sorrow. At church she held out ludicrously obvious signals of distress, to Walter's intense embarrassment and annoyance.

Mugford's second appeal was unmistakable and decisive.

"Sorry Maister 'Arriss ad'n cum up lately as 'e

promised. Polly took it very unkind. Wuz anything wrong between 'em?"

Walter at once recognised that things had now got beyond the stage when temporising would suffice. So at last he grasped the nettle firmly.

"Mr. Mugford," he said, not without a tremor in his voice, "you seem, I think, to be labouring under a—a misapprehension."

"Wat d'ye mean?" glared Mugford. "Wat d'ye mean?"

"Well, let's understand each other," said Walter; "you've evidently got an idea that I—a—I—a—well, that I came up to Great Barton especially to see your daughter."

"Well, wat if ye did? Nothin' to be ashamed uv in that, is there? She's a gel as most schulemaisters in the county would be ony tu glad to jump at." Mugford was getting angry.

"Yes, yes, Mr. Mugford, no doubt, no doubt; but what I'm trying to make you understand is that I *didn't* come up to the farm especially to see your daughter."

"Wat! D'ye mean to tell *me*——"

"You were very kind to me when I called, and so was Miss Mugford, and I was grateful. There the matter ends."

"Oh! there the matter ends, does it? There the matter ends! Wy, yew knows as 'ow yew come up a casting sheep's-eyes at my gel. Yew knows as 'ow yew encouraged 'er. Yew! Oi allus thought so quiet and straightforad!"

"Mr. Mugford, I beg you——"

"Oh, don't beg *me!* Yew'll 'ev to du the fair thing by my gel or yew'll know it."

"But, Mr. Mugford——"

"You needn't 'Mr. Mugford' *me!* Oi ain't to be caught wi' the sort o' chaff as my pore gel wuz; so don't try it on."

"But really, I assure you, you are entirely wrong. Miss Mugford will tell you herself, if you ask her." Walter was getting a trifle angry by this time.

"Oh! 'er ull, ull 'er! Oi *du* loike yewr cheek. Wy, the pore gel does nothin' but grizel, grizel, grizel, all day long at your shameful leavin' on 'er!"

This, for the moment, completely took the wind out of Walter's sails. But when he *did* recover himself he demonstrated with considerable vehemence the fact that he was about tired of the interview, and plumply told Mugford to go and hang himself, and take his precious daughter with him—which was distinctly insubordinate, and ungallant to boot.

The schoolmaster and the chairman of the Board

parted, each in what is usually described as a towering rage; and from that day Walter Harris's tenure of office at Chewton Bunney was unendurable to the last degree.

Mugford kept his daughter well in the background; there were future excursions to be considered. But he persecuted the schoolmaster with exquisite skill. He got the Board to put upon its Minutes all sorts of resolutions calculated to inflict the most galling indignities upon the young man. For one whose wits seemed so lumberingly heavy, he developed a real genius for persecution. For instance, chalk was no longer allowed the school by the box. By resolution of the Board it was to be obtained from the Clerk six sticks at a time! This was typical.

Walter still vented an occasional grumble at the condition of the attendance. By resolution, carried by four to one, it was resolved that Mr. Harris do call upon absentees himself out of school hours, and submit a report on his visitations every month to the Board.

This was the resolution, I fancy, which brought matters to a crisis. Walter's refusal to do this at the command of the Board took the form of three months' notice to leave. Being still well on the right side of thirty, and up-to-date in all his qualifications, he got a situation at Pendlebury-with-Markleigh—partly, I am glad to say, through the agency of Sneercombe the Inspector, and under a much more reasonable, if not an ideal, rural School Board.

But he scored off Mugford before he left in a way I should never have given him credit for.

All the time he had been at Chewton he had been corresponding with his bright particular College flame, Jessie Cross. Fortunately, Jessie wrote, after the manner of the New Woman, a distinctly masculine hand; so much so that one's natural inclination was to commence a reply to her, "Dear Sir."

Nay, so masculine was it, that neither Mrs. Copp at the post-office—who knew everybody's business from the fronts of the letters and the backs of the postcards—nor Mrs. Crump, had the slighest idea that those regularly received missives were associated so intimately with a very genuine affair of the heart. It was in this wise that the fact that Walter "had a young lady" was entirely unknown in Chewton.

And Jessie Cross couldn't understand why, of all things in the world, Walter should elect to be married at Chewton Church on the Saturday which followed the close of his engagement at the Board School. She would rather have had the event take place at home, in the church off the Rye Lane.

But Walter advanced two very good reasons.

He was anxious that Goodman should perform the ceremony, and he could scarcely ask him to take the journey to London for the purpose. In the second place, only a week would elapse between his leaving Chewton and taking up duties at Pendlebury. If, instead of his travelling up to London and down again, Jessie would agree to be married at Chewton, they could get in a full week's honeymoon at Ilfracombe.

All of which came to pass, Miss Jessie Cross setting Chewton all agog by arriving on the Friday afternoon in considerable circumstance. Mrs. Copp at the post-office took charge of the bride-elect for the night, and on the Saturday morning this "charming little wedding" took place, Mr. Hearty Goodman officiating.

I, who am merely an obscure rural in a neighbouring parish school, acted as "best man," and probably I alone of those present knew the meaning of the quiet, half-amused, half-reflective smile that stole now and again across the conventional bridegroom countenance.

For I alone knew that Walter had sent a cordial invitation to every member of the School Board to be present, and I knew that Mugford's was worded with exceptional profuseness.

Only, none of them put in an appearance; and Mugford, riding a couple of miles away across the country, brought his whip down viciously across the flank of his cob as the merry jangle of bells afar off caught his ears.

Half-soliloquising, Walter was heard by his young wife to say, towards the end of the next week, when thoughts of Pendlebury began to intrude, "Well, it'll prevent similar complications at Pendlebury, anyhow."

And thereafter followed an explanation, singularly veracious as explanations made under similar circumstances go.

They were both laughing boisterously as they disappeared round the Capstan Head.

IN THE MATTER OF A PARCHMENT ENTRY.

"My darling! don't give way. Sneakson is a—a—pig!"

The word snapped out viciously enough when it *did* come.

"I know how hard you've worked, and how dreadfully unfair this report is. But cheer up, old boy!"

And little Mrs. Stevens did her best to win her husband over to a calmer frame of mind.

"I shan't stand this, Nell. I'll see the brute—— *There! I've settled the matter!*"

And George Stevens threw his wife's scissors down so that the point of one of the blades stuck in the table as a strip of parchment fluttered to the ground.

"George! George! whatever have you done?"

"Done, girl? Can't you see? Cut out that swine's report. He shan't spoil *my* parchment, at any rate."

And George Stevens, white with rage, threw himself into a chair and covered his face with his hands.

For a moment there was silence, then a burst of hysterical tears upon George's neck, as the little woman broke down under contemplation of the dreadful tragedy which had just taken place.

And what was it? Let me tell you slowly whilst you brace yourself for the news. George Stevens had—cut—a—slice—from off—his parchment certificate!

Yes, indeed! Why the heavens didn't fall forthwith *I* don't know; they must have been too paralysed.

Now George Stevens, so far, had been a most successful teacher. No wonder. He was persevering, alert, up-to-date, and always had an eye open for new ideas and new notions. He was looked upon by his Board as a most promising young fellow, likely to rise to a Board Inspectorship, or the Head of a Higher Grade, or something of that sort.

His school was in a poorish district, but by dint of unceasing effort and the loyalty of a devoted staff he had managed to screw out some most praiseworthy results up to the present.

His Parchment entries gave evidence of his ability. And as the document now lies before me I can reproduce the entries as they stand. On the front page runs the legend that

"George Stevens, having been a student two years in the *Borough Road* Training College, was examined for a certificate and placed in the *First* division of candidates of the *Second* year. Also, That the above-named candidate, after having served the required period of probation in the *Milltown High Street Board* School, taught a class in the presence of Her Majesty's Inspector of Schools, who made the following Report: *G. Stevens' lesson was given with exceptional ability.* . . .

(Signed) "S. F. J. O'C. Brown,
H.M. Inspector."

"In order that this Certificate may serve as evidence of Practical Success, it may, after a period of ten years, be revised according to the character of the Inspectors' entries upon it.

"A. J. Mundella, *Vice-President.*"

Under this there was originally a stamp, but this is cut clean across, leaving nothing but the royal arms at the top, for the first leaf is now an inch and a half shorter than the second.

Over the page I get the following—

" First Inspection since last recorded date.

" *Milltown High Street Board* School, visited on the 23 of *November*, 1882. *Mr. Stevens' Class has passed a first-class examination.*

" S. J. F. O'C. Brown, *H.M. Inspector.*"

" Second Inspection.

" *Same* School, visited on the 24 of *November*, 1883.

" Again this very fine Upper Standard Class adds distinction to the school.

" S. J. F. O'C. Brown, *H.M. Inspector.*"

" Third Inspection.

" *Brickley, Alleywell Lane Board* School, visited on the 19 of *June*, 1884.

" Mr. Stevens opened this new school six months ago. The order is very good, and a satisfactory beginning has been made."

" W. W. Witson, *H.M. Inspector.*"

Fourth Inspection,

" *Same* School, visited on the 4 of *June*, 1885.

" The school is in most satisfactory condition.

" W. W. Witson, *H.M. Inspector.*

" Fifth Inspection.

" *Same* School, visited on 11 of *June*, 1886.

"I have again to report very favourably upon the school.

"W. W. WITSON, *H.M. Inspector.*"

"Sixth Inspection.

"*Same* School, visited on 18 of *June*, 1887.

"The school continues to make excellent progress.

"W. W. WITSON, *H.M. Inspector.*"

"Seventh Inspection.

"*Same* School, visited on 13 of *June*, 1888.

"I can again report most favourably upon the school.

"W. W. WITSON, *H.M. Inspector.*"

Here the record ends so far as this page is concerned, for the space whereon was written the report on the Eighth Inspection is cut clean away, and the top of the next page commences with a space for the Ninth Inspection, the page closing with space for the Sixteenth.

It was this Eighth Report which George Stevens, in a moment of passion, had cut off, and the reason therefor was the advent of a new Inspector in Brickley.

Sneakson they called him; and a man more unsuited to the work it would be difficult to conceive.

Sneakson had to live; and having no taste for the Church or the Army, they made him an Inspector of Schools in the twenty-fifth year of his age.

His first examination in Brickley—it was Jones's, of the National—is a thing terrible to recall. Jones has walked with a stick ever since. It was Sneakson's first time inside an elementary school: I leave you to imagine the rest.

I only want to say that, if Jones hadn't been spending the last thirty years of his energies getting grey and bent at school-teaching, Sneakson's head would have been broken on that occasion.

It is a pity it wasn't.

Six months later, after having "examined" some twenty schools, leaving behind him in each case much weeping amongst the women teachers and much bad language amongst the men, it became Sneakson's duty to visit Stevens' school, with the result that you have seen.

What the exact terms of the offensive Parchment entry were will never be known, unless somebody turns it up amongst the folios at Whitehall, where no doubt they have kept a copy. George burnt it directly he cut it off, and all I know is that it was something singularly insulting to a man of Stevens' record and standing. Of course, they had had three or four "tiffs" on the examination day, and this was Sneakson's particular method of taking his revenge.

By-and-by, little Mrs. Stevens got over her crying—it only started the children howling—and set about making some tea (women can always fall back upon the teacups if the worst comes).

From her husband's manner, she deemed it best to let him alone. Within a few minutes she was at his side, coaxing him to take a cup of tea. She knew better than to ask him to come to the table. Wonderful woman, little Mrs. Stevens!

"I shall report the matter at once, Nell," said George at last. "I could say nothing about it for a year; but when Sneakson asked for my Parchment next year it would all come out, and they would think I intended to commit a fraud in some way or other. You know what they are."

"Certainly, George; report the matter at once," was Mrs. Stevens' reply; but to whom he was to report it she was as profoundly ignorant as the two youngsters sitting at the tea-table on either side of her.

Thereat followed another long spell of silence.

"Nell," said the troubled man, after a time, "I think I'll go round and see Blakeley—see what *he* says."

And, the wife agreeing, Stevens took his hat and went out.

Within the hour he returned, and wrote a letter to Sneakson, enclosing the mutilated Parchment, telling him that he felt the last Report so unfair that, in a moment of passion, he had cut it out. He hastened to put the matter in the hands of the Inspector for the district.

Then they went to bed, both to lie for hours picturing a variety of sequels to this untoward circumstance.

There was no reply from Sneakson; but at the end of the week an official letter came from Whitehall to the effect that "the matter respecting the Parchment Certificate of G. Stevens, referred from C. H. Sneakson, Esq., H.M. Inspector of Schools, would receive early attention."

And George and his wife waited events.

Before the month was out the verdict came. The Clerk of the Brickley School Board was informed that in consequence of irregularities connected with an entry thereon, the Parchment Certificate of George Stevens, Certificated Master of the Second Class, had been suspended for a period of Five Years. Had it not been that the matter had been placed at once before the Department by George

Stevens himself, the penalty would have been more severe.

Walsh the Clerk came down post-haste to the school in a hansom to ascertain what on earth Mr. Stevens had been up to. It is pretty safe to say that no official communication ever made Walsh stare as this one did.

It was his bad fortune to be the first to break the news to Stevens, the Department not having condescended to communicate with him directly.

Perhaps I had better leave you to picture for yourselves how he received his sentence, and what Walsh said when he had the facts of the case placed before him.

At tea that evening little Mrs. Stevens saw at once that George was more than usually out of sorts; but she said nothing, thinking that it was the wringing agony of uncertainty.

"What should we do, Nell, old girl," at last said George, in an unsteady voice, "if they cancelled my Certificate?"

"Why, my dear boy," responded Nell, "they won't do *that*. Don't be down in the dumps; have some more tea. They'll give you a stiff caution, I should think—and serve you right, you hasty old tyrant. And it'll do you good!"

Nell Stevens was trying hard to be brave, and even light-hearted, but a close observer would have noticed that the corners of her mouth twitched a little in the process.

"I know, old woman; but just you think it out seriously," continued George. "What would become of us if they threw me out of work—say, for two or three years?"

"Oh! stuff and nonsense, you booby! Here, kiss Babs, and let me put her to bed."

And Nell Stevens held up a crowing, flaxen-haired little bundle of dancing delight, which the condemned man hugged in such a way as to make the mother snatch it away, fearful for the symmetry of the shoulder-knots.

It was a wistful look George Stevens threw after them as the pair went laughing out of the room, the complete personification of perfect happiness.

"Geordie, old chap," said Stevens, when his wife had returned, "go and ask Annie to let you have your engine off on the kitchen floor. I want to speak to Mams."

"Now, Nell," continued George, turning to his wife, "I *must* tell you what has happened. I seem to know you too well to be able to break it to you gently, though I've tried. Walsh had a letter to-day to say—— Here, come and sit on my lap, my pet."

"Yes, George, to say—— Tell me, my lad; I'm ready for the worst."

"Well, to say that my Certificate is——"

"Not *cancelled*, George!"

"No, my lass—not *that*. But suspended for five years!"

Nell sat upright, and looked out into the future across the little dining-room with set eyes and hands tight knotted around George's big fingers.

Then the brave little heart gave way, and she burst into hysterical tears.

"It's cruel! cruel! cruel!—after your slaving and grinding. God help us, George! What will become of the children?"

George gathered his wife to his arms, and by-and-by Nell sat up again composed and quiet, but looking many months older than five minutes earlier.

She went on in a steady voice—

"Why ever did we go away for the holidays?" (They had been to the seaside for three weeks, living at the rate of £600 a year on a salary of £225.) "Oh, if we had only known!

"Ay, ay, Nell—if we had only known!"

"What shall we do, George? We shall have to give up this house? You can't finish your payments to the Building Society now."

They had paid up £350 on a £450 house, and a grinding tyranny to them the process had been.

"Shall you leave Brickley? I could go home, and take the children with me, till you dropped into something."

And the little woman found solace in devising dozens of plans for meeting the crisis, each discarded for a new one, which only brought out more clearly than before the overwhelming nature of the blow which had befallen them.

To make a long story short, the Brickley School Board had no alternative but to dismiss their clever and esteemed young master, though they one and all sympathised with him and protested against the injustice of the sentence. A petition was sent to the Department from the Board and another from the teachers of the district, but all in vain. The head of the Department was inflexible.

A momentary glance at the case in the first stage of it, when Sneakson had sent it up, was sufficient to convince Sir Hardern Flint that fraud had been intended. Nothing so heinous had come under his notice for many years as the mutilation of a Government Parchment Certificate.

Why, the culprit ought to be at once hanged, drawn, and quartered! If this sort of thing were not put down with a severe hand—why, we should have every discontented teacher cutting strips out of his Parchment by way of obliterating distasteful entries.

At first Sir Hardern was for cancelling the Certificate right out: but there seemed to be a gleam of repentance in the fact that the man had voluntarily given himself up to justice, so he would make it a five years' suspension—and merciful enough that was in all conscience.

Wherefore no amount of petitioning effected any good; and George Stevens sold up his household gods—six years they had been getting them together, and things were only just getting straight—relinquished his interest in the house, and had to accept a shockingly unfair Surrender Value upon the little policy of life assurance he had taken out.

I have taken it for granted that everybody knows that the suspension of the man's Certificate debarred him, for the time being, from working in an elementary school. If you are not aware of the fact, I present it you, my gentle patron, as the sort of thing that justifies the universal belief in the Englishman's sense of fair play.

Little Mrs. Stevens and the children went down to Oakappleton to the old people, and lived on next to nothing, for the very excellent reason that they had next to nothing to live on.

And George hung about Brickley and enjoyed the privilege of entering into the state of mind of the leper without suffering his physical disability, which, in the way of experience, is worth trying for the space of something inside of a week.

You say, "Why did he stay at Brickley?" I say, What could he have done elsewhere? For five long years he dared not show his nose near the only work for which he was fitted. He was as well and as badly off at Brickley as anywhere else.

Besides, he had some sympathisers in Brickley. Jones, the member of the Board who was a solicitor, gave him some copying work to do. I will not breathe a syllable as to what Jones paid him, because I want Jones to remain canonised for all time for his ready assistance. Then he addressed envelopes at three shillings per thousand; acted as general utility man to an auctioneer; went out "private teaching" once or twice a week; and, in short, scraped a living in a hundred odd ways.

Oh! it is a merry time for the schoolmaster out of collar. He can turn his hand to so many things!

Occasionally he was able to send five shillings' worth of stamps to his wife; but it was only *very* occasionally, and it was a good job that her father and mother were alive and able to keep a roof-tree over the heads of their daughter and two grandchildren.

But all this was six years ago. For there was in Brickley one Sleeman, a corn-dealer; and for Sleeman George drew up a Circular one day, after he had been "out" about a year. Sleeman was so delighted with the style of the thing and George's general demeanour —it must have been his demeanour, because his hat and coat and boots wouldn't have been much of a warranty even amongst crossing-sweepers—that Sleeman asked him if he would come daily and do some writing and figuring.

Which certainly he would; and he did, with so much good effect that Sleeman shortly afterwards took him on permanently in his office at the princely wage of thirty shillings a week.

Six months with Sleeman set George Stevens on his legs again, and the shrewd corn-factor quickly set those legs a-going by putting the whilom schoolmaster on the road for him in what Sleeman called his South-Western District.

Then it was that Nellie Stevens and Babs and Geordie came out of exile, and there was a happy evening for the people at No. 6, Henry Street.

Before George had been twelve months with Sleeman he saw plainly enough that his career as a teacher was over for good; and many a time he has since said to me—who never had the pluck to cut a snip out of his Parchment, and who therefore remains grinding on with book and duster and chalk—"Ah, my dear Blakely, if a young chap only put half the energy, endeavour, and zeal into business that the average teacher is compelled to put into his school, in ten years he would be well on the way to fortune."

To which I as many times said "Amen!" devoutly.

George Stevens is not exactly on the way to his fortune just yet. But he is Sleeman's smartest representative, and what with salary and commission easily earns more than he ever aspired to in the service of the Brickley School Board.

Did he get his Parchment back at the end of the five years? Yes, and before that; for there came a change in the heads of the Education Office, and the new chief, coming across the case accidentally one day, went into it himself. They tell me that he used somewhat forcible language; directed George's Parchment to be at once returned to him; and, further, went so far as to say very handsomely that if the

Department could help George in any way to get into a school again it would most decidedly do so.

Happily, George stood in no need of either the Parchment or the Department's tardy restitution. But he is never tired of acknowledging the new man's action, nevertheless.

Three months ago some of us, George's old colleagues, approached him about a matter not altogether unconnected with school work. And he consulted Sleeman, who readily agreed.

With the result that a fortnight ago last Thursday "George Stevens, traveller," headed the poll for the Brickley School Board by an overwhelming vote above the next man on the list; for Brickley had not forgotten the dirty trick of 1889.

I am looking forward to a good time for Sneakson. So is he!

FADDY, H.M.I.

"INSPECTION sore long time I bore" shall be my epitaph when I have vindicated my claim to the title "Elementary" by shuffling off this mortal coil and returned to my original "elements."

With head in the noose of pedagogic drudgery, and back bent to the thraldom of inspectorial yoke, I have but little time to do aught but grin and bear Faddy's vagaries; yet it would be a pity if the world were never to know the story of his little eccentricities, pleasantries, and idiosyncrasies. Let the task be mine, therefore.

There are those who tell me that in society he is an extremely harmless and amiable sort of fellow; and, indeed, it would be difficult, in a crowd, to single him out as being in any sense elevated by personal ability above the general rut of mediocre nonentity. It is only when invested, as he is in his capacity as "H.M.I.," with despotic power that he becomes dangerous, and even then it is often unwitting and unintentional on his part.

It is no particular fault of his that he is the son of his father, and *that* father related, by a long line of " his uncles and his cousins and his sisters and his aunts," to some member of a former Government; and it must be taken as his misfortune rather than his fault that, up to the time of his being commissioned to write the magic letters H.M.I. after his patronymic, he was sweetly innocent of ever having crossed the threshold of an " Elementary " school!

To some it may be a matter for surprise that the " Elementary " teachers did not object to provide the *corpus vile* upon which the sucking Inspector must necessarily have tried his 'prentice hand. Perhaps they feared lest worse things should come upon them. Or was it that they had piously read their Leviticus and had come to the conclusion that *now*, as under the Old Dispensation, there must be a sacrifice for the sins of ignorance; and that it was meet and proper that they themselves, in their own persons, should provide the sacrifice, the more so since it was necessary that the sacrifice must be without spot or blemish?

Transformed as Faddy was from the Graduate in Arts, with his eye-glass, his lackadaisical insipidity, and his aristocratic drawl, by one single " Hey! presto!" into a full-blown journeyman Inspector, and transplanted as he was into a new world with a new and strange species of human life, who can wonder that Faddy floundered? Could it be expected that he should ever rise to a broad and intelligent grasp of his calling? Should surprise be expressed if he groped helplessly along in the mire of mere mechanical details? How much of the real aims and true aspects of education could his inexperienced mediocrity bring within its gaze?

When he made his bow, arrayed in Inspectorial authority, dire was the gloom that fell upon the "Elementary" ones of the district, whose educational destiny and possibilities it was, from that time forth, his peculiar privilege to rule—and to mar. Many an "Elementary" one set his teeth and dug his nails into the palms of his hands at the sight of the year's monument of toil and self-sacrifice shattered by the single blow of amateur incapacity.

In those days he was wont to come up smilingly, "with an eye-glass in his ocular," to the younkers of eight years, and sweetly and suavely drawl out: "Now, children, what is the function of a verb?" varied by "What proof positive have we, children, of the rotundity of the globe?" or "What is the nature, boys, of a river?"

It was not—and I speak feelingly—a pleasant sight to see the look of blank astonishment, followed by the dull gaze of careless inattention, which fell as a blight upon even my most forward seedlings, as he meandered on his course of dissertative inquiry—a course rarely interrupted by anything he ever got in the shape of response from the hopefuls under his gaze, and a course which he himself invariably terminated by turning to me with a sweet smile—"It is clearly obvious that this work has not been done!"

But that eye-glass! What human computation shall gauge the havoc played by that iniquitous eye-glass! Ye Trojans of old, paralysed as ye were by the approach of that one-eyed *monstrum horrendum*, thank Heaven that at three years of age ye came not under Faddy's eyeglass! Under its mysterious spell my saplings relapsed into a helplessly stricken and semi-comatose condition, and naught would avail to rouse them.

And his superfine accent! Who shall measure the disaster spread among youthful orthographers by his fearful parody of pronunciation? I have stood beside him passively whilst he has done his best to wreck my hopes by dictating "water" as "watah"! "proper" as "propah"! and "culture" as "cultchaw"! He might have finished it, and turned pathetically to me and smiled "paw beggah!"

In the early days of his inspectorship Faddy was, as I have said, fearful to contemplate, and withal, poor man! like King Gama, I daresay he often told himself, "I can't tell why." I have seen him riddle a few ragged urchins of ten summers fore and aft with the different aspects of the three verbs "to lay," "to lie" (to lie down), and "to lie" (to tell a lie), until the poor chaps and myself were well-nigh fit to be "laid out."

It may be uncharitable to mention it, but in the early days of his departmental dignity he was not particularly distinguished for too close an acquaintance with the intricacies of the "New Code of Regulations," for he had a child-like way of wandering up and down the whole gamut of knowledge in the particular subject under examination. I sometimes "pulled him up," but his invariable reply was: "Quite so, Mr. X——; I am fully aware that I am going beyond the requirements, but the boys have satisfied me that they know the portions prescribed for them, and I want to see if they know anything *beyond* that." It was always well, however, to "pull him up"; for if one allowed him to ramble on, he would get very few answers, of course, and would go away with a vague notion that the boys did not know their work; and this vague notion would have settled down into a firm conviction by the time he sat down at home to write his report of the school.

Time's whirligig has gone round many a time since he and I first crossed swords, and we have grown old and grey together. He is ruddier, and heavier, and of a more well-favoured appearance than of yore, and his self-satisfied complacency indicates the easy-going ambler through life. As for me—ah! well, I have been "lighting a candle to knowledge," and wrinkles gather apace at the task. I do not hear nowadays of Faddy's frequent infringing of the Code; he has felt his feet as to the minutiæ of inspection, but is quite innocent of ever having made the slightest attempt to compass the highest dignity of his calling and by no stretch of imagination could he be termed an educationalist.

Much of the real work of examination is done by his drudging assistants—who get a couple of hundreds a year to his seven-fifty—whilst he, good soul! pokes about here and there, like a careful housewife in search of dust. The simile is the more apt because some call him "an old woman," and aver that he is "full of fads"; but of that I will not presume to offer an opinion.

If this should, however, meet the eye of an "Elementary" one whose altogether lovely task it is annually to endeavour to satisfy Faddy's whims in the winter or early spring, let me earnestly entreat him to have the schoolroom *warm, very warm*, on the auspicious occasion of his visit. By no means, however, must the atmosphere be in that condition colloquially known as "stuffy."

It will be almost impossible for the "Elementary" one, to whom my remarks are addressed, to keep up heat enough for Faddy without seriously vitiating the air; but as my reader values his peace of mind, let him not abandon the task without a struggle: 89·9° Fahr. exactly—not one decimal point above or below—will do it. Vary this in the slightest and Faddy's greeting will be, "Deah me! what a close atmosphere!" (emphasised by a series of ejaculatory sniffs), or "Deah me! how dweadfully cold this woom is; I shall be pewished!" (accompanied by a series of shrugs and grimaces that would do credit to a Laplander), and my "Elementary" friend will hear whichever of these Faddy opens with every time he comes near him for the rest of the day.

His next whine of querulous discontent is, "Deah me! how dahk this woom is!" or "Deah me! what a glare of light you have!" and the poor ubiquitous pedagogue is responsible for sun, moon, stars, rain, hail, thunder, lightning, and whatever else happens in any part of the universe during the rest of Faddy's visit.

He is, too, a judge of "marching," be it observed. I have never yet seen a file of boys march past him without "Deah me! how badly those boys maach! They should move no muscles except those of the legs, and not those if they can help it!"

Another favourite and invariable attack of his is: "Deah me! how badly those boys waise their hands to answah a question! One and all must waise the *wight* hand—so" (suiting the action to the word by sticking his right elbow into his ribs and spasmodically elevating the right forearm, fingers extended, after the manner affected by farthing wooden dolls). Then he turns to the boys and says: "Boys, look at me. Nevah lean fo'wad to answah a question; sit *quite* still, and waise the wight hand so—always the wight hand, nevah the left, gently—so" (dumb show *da capo*).

May we leave Faddy here for the present, wagging his arm up and down? He is appropriately occupied.

FOR THE HONOUR OF THE NATION.

". . . . . . So I gave him ink and paper and let the old chap write out the story of his grievances, promising to send them on to you, sir, as the member for the division. I don't know what you can do, but the putting together of enclosed has eased his mind a bit. . . ."

THE covering letter was addressed to my very good friend the member for the Soliham division of Westawayshire, and knowing my interest in educational affairs he asked me to look through the enclosure and advise him upon the matter. I took the liberty to copy out the old man's petition, altering only the names of persons and places. It is written in a curiously neat hand. Some of the longer strokes are eloquent of old age, but that is so common as to pass almost unnoticed. The remarkable feature is the width of the letters in some lines and words, their narrowness in others. There can be no harm now in making the contents public :—

"Dec. 23rd, 1894.

"HONOURED SIR,—I desire most respectfully to lay the facts concerning my case before you. Fifty years ago I was head boy in the first class at the Church of England School for the parish of Byeway-in-the-Woods, near Collywell, county Durham. It was intended by my parents that I should become a farrier, but one day, just before arrangements were finally made, Mr. Merrifield, the vicar, came into school and asked the Master (Mr. Ball) whether he didn't think I should make a good teacher.

"Mr. Ball said he did, only he had understood that my parents had pretty well completed arrangements, he thought, for my apprenticeship to the farriery.

"'Oh,' said Mr. Merrifield, 'that'll be all right. I'll see Mr. Stokes'—meaning my father—'to-night.'

"And, sir, this he did.

"I remember the evening as well as if it were yesterday; for my father, being a just man, called me in, and said as the business concerned me most closely I had better be present and hear what was going on.

"Mr. Merrifield had brought down with him a printed document, endorsed on the back, as you will see, sir—'Minutes of the Committee of Council on Education, August and December, 1846.'

"I beg to enclose a copy of the same, which was afterwards sent to me direct from the Education Department, Whitehall. My father also had a copy sent direct to him. I have marked page 6 referring to the prospect of a retiring pension at the end of my career.

"It was this prospect which, upon Mr. Merrifield's representation, induced us to give up the farriery idea and take up teaching."

[Here is duly filed the copy of the Minute of 21st December, 1846. The marked portion of page 6 reads:—

Retiring Pensions to School Masters and Mistressses for long and efficient Services.

That a retiring pension may be granted by the Committee of Council to any schoolmaster or schoolmistress who shall be rendered incapable, by age or infirmity, of continuing to teach a school efficiently.

Provided that no such pension shall be granted to any schoolmaster or schoolmistress who shall not have conducted a normal or elementary school for fifteen years, during seven at least of which such school shall have been under inspection.

That in all cases of application for pensions a report shall be required from the Inspector, and from the Trustees and Managers of the schools, as to the character and conduct of the applicants, and the manner in which the education of the pupils under their charge has been carried on.

The amount of the pension shall be determined according to such report, but shall in no case exceed two-thirds of the average amount of the salary and emoluments annually received by the applicant during the period that the school has been under inspection.

A minute of the grant of every such pension and of the grounds on which it has been awarded shall be published in their Lordships' Minutes.]

"Well, sir, I was duly apprenticed, as you will see from the enclosed forms, my indentures dating from June 1st, 1847."

[Here follow copy of indenture, also original Agreement, endorsed on the back "Byeway-in-the-Woods Church of England School: dated this first day of June, 1847. George Henry Crook Merrifield to Ralph Robert Wheeler Lingen, Esq. Agreement to repay Stipends and Gratuities on interruption of school or refusal of Inspection."]

"After five years' work I went for one year to the Normal School at Chelsea, leaving there in 1853.

"I at once entered upon my duties as a Government teacher, taking charge of the Blue Coat School at Lambfield, at a salary of £30 a year and house rent-free.

"This, sir, was in January, 1854, and I worked

at Lambfield for fifteen years without a day's absence, going in 1869 to the National School at Chirley, in Westawayshire, at a commencing salary of £55 a year, two-thirds of the grant, and house and garden. I worked on at Chirley, sir, for twenty-two years without a break, making in all, as you will see, thirty-seven years' continuous service.

"I need not trouble you with the fact that in the year of my going to Chirley I married. Nor need I unnecessarily lengthen this letter, which is trespassing upon your kind consideration and patience far too much already, by telling you how, nine years later, my wife and our three little ones were carried off by scarlet fever, due, I shall contend to my dying day, to the state of the school-house.

"What I want to tell you is that after the death of my wife and children, living all alone as I was, and always having been of a most careful disposition, I managed to lay by, year by year, my share of the grant, until, in 1891, I had to my credit at the Westaway County Bank the splendid sum of £300.

"Sir, my eyesight had begun to fail me—I am almost stone-blind now, and have to guide one hand with the other to keep straight with the edge in writing—and in every way I was fast becoming very enfeebled; and having rendered thirty-seven years' faithful service I decided to lay down my book and pen and give place to a younger man, rejoicing in the assurance that, with my £300 in the bank and my Government pension, I should be able to eke out my last few solitary days in comparative comfort.

"So I sent up for my pension, when, to my complete surprise and consternation, I was directed to the entry I had made on the Application Form respecting my £300 in the bank, and was told that, having this amount at my disposal, I could not be considered eligible for a Government pension!

"Sir, I will ask you to turn back to page 6, of the first paper enclosed, and read the marked portion again. Is there any reference there to my savings? Was I, who had been expected to inculcate habits of thrift all my life, to be so cruelly punished now *because of my own thrift?*

"I did not look for the two-thirds of my average salary" spoken of on page 6 of the first paper; I knew *that* pledge had already gone to the winds. But in the name of justice I expected one of the twenty, twenty-five, or thirty pound pensions which are granted to teachers who, like myself, entered under the Minute of December 21st, 1846.

"Sir, I was thunderstruck. But I had to grin and bear it; and, at any rate, thanked God for my economies of the previous thirteen years.

"As I have said, my eyes were failing fast; I was enfeebled; I could not keep pace with the latest Codes; and although I failed to get my pension, my managers were compelled, so they put it, to ask me to resign.

"I did resign—in December, 1891—and took a room in the village, granting myself a monthly allowance at a rate that would make my savings see me to the end.

"Sir, you will remember the 7th of April, 1893. It was a Friday—for me a terribly Black Friday; for on that day the Westaway County Bank failed, and closed its doors. How could a poor old solitary man like me, half-blind and too feeble to rush off quickly, find a place amongst the few who saved themselves whilst the doors were closing?

"I was ruined and friendless! No, not friendless. My old scholars came one by one and pressed my hand in the fulness of their hearts. But what could *they* do, with fifteen shillings at the best, and many hungry mouths to be fed?

"Sir, I had to come here. God help me! It was *that* or starvation. I have been here now a year and eight months. If I had been a drunkard, a spendthrift, or a vagabond, I should not feel it, maybe. But it is *very* hard for an old man like me—harder, sir, than I can tell you. The master and his wife are kindness itself. If it had been otherwise, I should have died long since.

"I have written this long and wearisome letter to you because I have always heard them speak of you as a kind gentleman, and one willing to help the distressed. I do not ask for money—Heaven forbid!—but what I beg of you to do is to go to the Education Department and tell them of the bank failure. Tell them I *can't* die here. Entreat them to save me.

"Sir, I hope you will forgive me for this long letter and this trouble. I have no claim to impose this on you. Yet my dreadful state must plead my forgiveness.

"I beg respectfully to remain
    "Your obedient servant,
        "SAMUEL STOKES."

Such are the terms of the old man's letter, conveyed to my very good friend the member for Soliham through the kindness of the Master of the Workhouse of the Soliham Union, Westawayshire.

Not more than half-a-dozen sentences of mine were necessary to make him understand the bearings of the case; nor had half-a-dozen hours elapsed before he was filling in an Interview Form at the Education Office, in Whitehall.

That his plea was listened to with genuine kindliness will not require the telling for all those who know the genial sympathetic Chief who rules there. Neither is there much need to add that at the next allocation of pensions at Lady-Day last, the old man got his thirty pounds, and we took him back to the room wherein he had hoped to end his days.

He had not exhausted his first seven pounds ten before his last wish was granted. But I shall never cease to rejoice that he did not die in the Workhouse.

My friend the member for the Soliham division will get no glory for the little service he rendered the old schoolmaster. There was no paragraph in the local papers about it; but I am not sure that it will not count for righteousness far more than much politics.

THE CRISIS AT PETTI-FOGGERINGTON.

"I votes as 'ow us sacks her right off! Right off, I repeats, wi'out notice. She's a darned sight too much o' the fine lady to suit my barrel, so I tells y'h!"

It was a meeting of the School Board for the United District of Petti-Foggerington and Great Drivellingham, and little Spriggs the cobbler—who headed the poll at the last election — was the spokesman.

"Sir!" continued Spriggs, waxing warm, "you knaws as well as I do 'ow 'er tried to get you into a row last 'arvest over them there Smallses as 'ow you had out in the fields a-saving 'ay; and a blessin' to their parents it was, that there 'arf-a-crown a week you paid the fower on 'em. O' course, you carn't expect a young 'Oity-toighty o' the likes o' she to understand the bearings o' these yer questions. All you can expect 'er to do is to try to get the Guvment Expecter to get us into trouble with her knowing ways—which her ups and does—which again I seys her ought to go right off!

Now wat's the latest? Why, yer we are, robbed of ten pun odd by the Heddycashunal Partishun in London. And for w'y? I asks. For w'y? Becos we give way to 'er and give 'er a hextra girl to 'elp 'er. For which, I repeats, we be robbed by them as is in London, and knaws nort abawt it, for 'avin' too much staff in the schule! Which no more of it I'll stand. I votes again, Sir, that 'er goes right off! That's all I got to say."

"Mister Cheerman"—this with a peculiarly raucous snuffle—"I begs to give my 'arty support to our worthy friend's words. I don't say as 'ow she bain't a wery gude schule-taicher. I don't say that, mind you. Far from it. But what I *does* say is that she comes it too thick for volks like us. Her makes out that schuling be everything. Which I never had a day's buke-larnin' in my life! Us can't 'ave the boys in the fields when us wants 'em, becos' they bain't a passed Sempshun Standerd or wat 'er calls it. And now us reads in this yer report which 'ave just a come to 'and that the closet drains want a-lookin' arter! Which I reckon thirty pun and more will be gone at one bang afore we've a dun wi' this ere darned job!

"Why, yer be I, the biggest varmer in the parish or anywheres this side o' Little Bickerington, wi'out any drains at all! Too much folderol goin' on nowadays, I says. I bain't the man to make a long sarmon, as you knows; so I jest ses 'Yer, yer!' to Mr. Spriggs' words, and that is that 'er clears out at once!"

And "Varmer" Maggs resumed his seat with a self-satisfied grunt.

Kate Parrington, you must know, left the British and Diocesan Training College as nearly as may be a year ago, to take charge of the little village school in Petti-Foggerington. Imbued with the loftiest purpose, bearing away from her College home all the highest and best of educational ideals, and blessed with a strong physique and a merry heart, she came to the work at Petti-Foggerington thoroughly determined to allow no obstacle to stand between her and success, to permit no anxiety to dishearten her, and to tolerate no difficulty as insurmountable.

Kate had been at the work ten short months only, and yet she stood outside in the schoolroom amongst her charges this dreary December afternoon sick and tired at heart, her spirit completely crushed, her ideals shattered, and her temper bitterly soured.

She had put her whole soul into her work, and her heart ached for the want and destitution which the flabby, bloodless lips and faces of the little ones around her silently indicated. Before Easter she had come to a sudden resolve to throw the examination—which was then some six months due—to the winds, and think of nothing but the succouring of the starving minds and bodies entrusted to her care.

What would happen when the Great Man came—and she had heard disquieting rumours of his autocratic and overbearing manner—she soon began to feel too thoroughly disheartened to care. All she could endeavour to achieve was a poor and feeble ministering to the daily crying needs of the wretched scraps of humanity around her.

And so she toiled on, abused most by certain of the parents when she was working her hardest for their neglected offspring.

At night she shared a squalid bedroom—the staircase of which led, without landing or other protection, at once into the room below—with the widow of a labourer, whose lot was such that early morn and darkening eve saw her in the fields toiling in a pair of her late husband's heavy, mud-bedaubed, hobnailed boots. Below there was, it is true, a stone-flagged dwelling-room, but up to Easter Kate could only sit in it crouched before the fire and wrapped in her warmest winter cloak.

So uncongenial were the only lodgings the village

offered, that until the summer came she sat alone in the dimly-lighted schoolroom, cooking her scanty meals at the fire herself, and listening in exquisite terror to the soughing of the trees outside the farthest window or to the scratching of a mouse in the darkest corner.

When spring, however, had lighted up the dark places and loosened the rigid bonds of winter, things became more endurable. There were white and scented violets to seek; primroses to pluck for the window of the little school and her own white-washed bedroom window-ledge; and, above all, there were the Lenten lilies to look for in the moist, green corners fretted out by the little brook in its wayward journeyings.

And as spring beamed into summer, Kate almost put away, as a terrible nightmare, the recollections of those dark, cruel months now happily behind her.

Meanwhile her daily work at the school was rapidly knocking all that was best and brightest out of her constitution.

Month by month a little coterie of bigoted illiterates, calling themselves "the Schule Booard," met in the little class-room where they are at this moment.

To these meetings Kate looked forward with a dread that quickly developed into abject fear. This, in its turn, ultimately became tinctured with a keen and bitter strain of cynicism and hatred. From these meetings Kate went home—not cheered and encouraged, not stimulated for the month's struggle before her—but with a burning head, an insulted spirit, and an eyelash that was hot with stifled tears.

I am not going into all the petty tyrannies practised by the miserably narrow-minded little set of contemptible humbugs calling themselves her masters. Most of my readers can, unfortunately, imagine them only too well.

A terrible row had taken place at the re-assembling of the school after the Midsummer holiday, Kate flatly telling the members that she would write at once to the Inspector for the district if they persisted in employing pupils of seven years of age and in Standard I. "leading horses," and of eight and nine years of age and in Standards II. and III. "binding" and "saving."

She had put her foot down, and they had caved in, breathing out a strongly aromatic vengeance upon her over their tumbler-ful of shrub-rum in the back parlour of "The Pig and Porker," where they were wont to adjourn after every monthly meeting.

October brought the Government Inspector on that stupid—ay, and oftentimes cruel—annual errand of his, the Government Examination of her little school.

Old Faddy, as a result of a life-time of autocracy which had battened unhealthily upon indiscriminate adulation, had become a thorough-paced tyrant, in manner, at any rate. But he was not a bad fellow at heart by any means; and when up at Oxford in the 'Forties, he was universally admitted to be a really decent sort of chap—"no brains, you know"—and, what more than made up for this deficiency in the estimate of the Undergrad, no "side" either.

Faddy was the last man who should have developed into a crotchety, fidgety, autocratic old martinet.

And yet he did; which only goes to show under what wretchedly bad conditions he received his training. I think his title, "Her Majesty's Inspector," helped him to go wrong. If he had been a plain "Inspector," he would probably have kept more humble. But you can't expect a man who carries about the title "Her Majesty's Inspector" to have any other than a high stomach, can you?

Then again (I blush to write it) certain teachers had conspired to spoil Faddy by much lick-spittling, to use a highly expressive, if somewhat ojectionable, term. I know of one lady teacher who always arranged the table, artistically covered with flowers, near the stove. By the side of the table was Faddy's chair, ready for him, all nicely warmed; and from the chair to each class ran strips of stair-carpet, so that he might not step upon anything so plebeian as an uncarpeted school-floor! More than that, as it was not possible—the schoolroom being so narrow—to pass *behind* Faddy's table, it was necessary now and again to pass between the wind—I mean, the class—and his nobility. Whenever a pupil-teacher or assistant did so, it was always with a deep obeisance and a muttered "Excuse me, sir," delivered with an embarrassed, frightened air.

At midday Faddy, who was examining a class in reading, was seen to throw down his book with a loud disgust-denoting "Faugh!" get up and walk to the other end of the room to relieve his feelings. Nobody seemed to be able to suggest the slightest reason for this outburst of temper (the class then under examination could read better than any in the school), and Miss Cent-per-center talked for a long time about appealing to the N. U. T. She would have done so, too, only she had begun to think of next year's examination, and *that* took her mind off Faddy's unconscionable exhibition of caprice.

Well, Faddy examined Kate's school in October,

and, I am bound to say, took the situation in with a breadth of mind for which I had not given him credit. He spoke kindly to Kate, who had strung herself up for the worst battle of all, and in kindly, fatherly tones expressed the warmest sympathy with her in the many anxieties and difficulties which he well knew surrounded her.

And when at last she burst into tears, he turned sharply away and talked pretty straight to "Varmer" Bushel, the Cheerman of the Booard, who stood by with an idiotic simper upon the unabashed breadth of cheek which served him for a countenance.

Kate went home that night with a lighter heart than for many a weary day previously, and old Mrs. Parrington—who had given up her lodgings in Kennington to come down to Petti-Foggerington when her daughter returned after the harvest holiday, with the winter before her—saw at once, as she hovered about the toast and tea-cakes, significant of the great occasion, that the day had gone better than had been expected. There was a touch of the girl's old cheery self that night in the little cottage next the blacksmith's; but the Parringtons would scarcely have felt so easy in their minds if they could have put on Gygës' ring and looked in at the back parlour of "The Pig and Porker" unobserved.

The village cronies had foregathered for the night, and Bushel was there, indignant at Mr. Faddy's criticism of the policy of the School Board for the United District of Petti-Foggerington and Great Drivellingham. Darkly only hinted he at the episode touching the schoolmistress, but Spriggs the cobbler "made no two ways about 'er bein' at the bottom uv it." Bushel was not the man to spare a woman's good name, certainly. He was counted a tyrant by all who came near him; and, indeed, it was only fifteen months since he had laid his own wife in her grave, the victim of his ungovernable brutality. Still, with a drunken leer, he "thought as 'ow Spriggs might as well let the schulemissus alone for once." At ten the choice spirits tumbled out into the night, ravishing the black silence with loud guffaws and spluttering tallow lanterns.

Thus the incident of the examination day. And now the report had come down, and the "Booard" is meeting in the little class-room critically weighing it over.

Faddy had paid a warm tribute to the excellent influence Miss Parrington had exercised, and had gone on to hope for good fruit for the future if she received the proper amount of support from the members of the Board The school, however, was fined some ten pounds under "the 17s. 6d. limit"; the drainage wanted attention; and " My Lords " would treat severely any further infraction of the Board's bye-laws such as certain entries in the log-book during the past year had disclosed.

And, as you have heard, Spriggs the cobbler has put it all down to Miss Parrington's influence with the Inspector, and has moved her immediate dismissal. This Maggs has seconded, whilst a third farmer has given the suggestion support, vehement if somewhat involved.

"Let's 'ave 'er in," chimes in Spriggs again, " and give 'er a bit uv our minds!"

"Yer, yer," say the others, with the exception of Chairman Bushel, who rises deliberately, and with a show of circumstance and importance.

" Genelmen," he says, " I quite agrees with all you've a said; but us 'ad better be careful. You remembers wat 'appened over at Little Duffington? Very well, genelmen, Miss Parrington's a member uv this yer Union too, and us 'ad better do the thing in reg'lar form. Us don't want no lawyer chaps from Lunnon a-worritting *us*, I reckons? If you like, I'll step out and ask 'er about these yer points in the report, and see wat 'er 'as to say."

A grunted approval, a click at the primitive door-latch, a flood of light from the paraffin lamp suspended from the class-room rafter, and Bushel has stumped out into the darkening schoolroom. The children have gone, the room is empty. The mistress stands alone at the little stove, awaiting her masters' pleasure.

Bushel has closed the class-room door, and now came forward to where the girl stands aimlessly waiting.

"I'm a cum to ask ye about this yer report. Us takes it badly, I can tell ye, after paying you the wages us 'ave a dun"—[£50 a year all told, by the way]—"for you to put th' Inspector on to us like as this is!"

Poor girl! she had vainly allowed herself to fancy that her masters would have congratulated her on the improved grants earned, and on the kindly references to her good influences and endeavours.

It was a rude awakening. But she might have known better; and gulping down a rising lump of disappointment, she said as quietly as she could command, "What do you mean, Mr. Bushel?"

"Wat do I mean? Wat do I mean?" retorted Bushel excitedly. "Cum, now, I likes that! W'y, about them there drains, and that there money we've a bin robbed of, and that there bye-law bisness!"

"Really, Mr. Bushel, I don't know what you mean. Mr. Faddy put those things down because they required attention. About the robbery you speak of, I don't understand the thing myself," replied the girl, still quietly, but with a breaking voice.

"Now, none of yer nonsense," snarled Bushel warmly. "You put him up to all that. You knaws you did; so you might as well out with it straight; let's 'ave no more shilly-shally."

"Mr. Bushel"—and the voice had become firm and hard in that moment—"you forget yourself. I have told you already I know nothing about it. I will wish you good-night."

"Nay, not so fast, my beauty," hissed Bushel, getting between the girl and the door.

"Let me pass, sir," the girl demanded again, in a firm and steady voice, shrinking back as she stood from the vicious gleam in the man's eyes and the hot foulness of his breath on her cheek.

"Not so fast, my fine schulemissus," growled the farmer in a guttural whisper between his teeth. "Yer—d'ye know we're goin' to sack ye? Ay, I thought that 'ud fetch ye to!" as the girl visibly staggered, and caught the rail of the little gallery for support. Not of herself did she think, though the ruin of her brightest hopes flashed through her distraught mind as she grasped the situation. It was her aged and lonely mother that rose before her instantly and unconsciously.

"I thought that 'ud fetch ye to!" he repeated, speaking thickly and rapidly. "But listen! I've allus a stuck up for ye, or you'd a been turned out of this long enough ago. You knaws *that*, right enough. And I'll stand by ye now if ye'll promise—there, I'm not a man of many words"—but he hesitated for a moment, as the girl braced herself up and looked him fixedly in the eye—"if ye'll promise—to—to—

"Pshaw!" he spluttered out, as if ashamed of his own hesitancy, "if ye'll promise to change yer name for Bushel! There you are; it's out now, and you can be the biggest farmer's wife for twenty mile around as soon as ye like."

It was well that Bushel talked on after his offer, or he would have seen that which would have made him dangerous. As it was, Miss Parrington, with that inborn adaptability of mind which is woman's most effective protection, had got the whole thing over before he finished. The first rush of disgust had left her strangely calm and equable, though words were scarcely at her command as readily as she could have wished. "I—I—I really—I——. But we were talking about the report," she stumbled out.

"Oh, hang the report!" blustered Bushel. "There, that's all settled then, and I'll go back and pull ye through."

"No, no, no! Mr. Bushel, you do not understand. You——" cried the girl, really excited now.

"Oh, all right; don't make any fuss. I'll manage that easy enough." And before she could stop him a gleam from the class-room sent a triangle of warm light across the floor.

The girl staggered back out of it; the door had closed, and she was again alone.

What should she do? Her thoughts came rapidly enough now, and she felt herself vile in their possession.

Hastily she snatched up her hat and cloak, and almost before they were donned she was away across the black, puddly school-yard, and down the pitch-dark, uneven lane to the cottage next the blacksmith's. A white band of light from the open door marks the limit of her journey. There, all regardless of the biting December wind, is her mother.

Mrs. Parrington is strangely elated; for, good soul! as a rule she takes the valley of life with enviable equanimity. So elated, indeed, is she that she does not notice her daughter's distracted air, for which the girl will never cease to be thankful.

"Oh, Kitty, whatever *do* you think? I had almost come up to the school to tell you, but the roads are so wet; and I was afraid to give one of the children the letter, for fear it should be lost."

"Yes, yes, mother; what is it, what is it?" cried the breathless girl.

"There, there; don't be so excited. That is always your way, as I am always telling you."

"Yes, yes, I know! Go on! go on!" again ejaculated the girl. "Here, mums, give it to me; you'll never get through it!" And the girl ran into the room to read the letter at the lamplight, whilst her mother followed with uplifted hands and a *sotto voce* "Was there *ever* such a girl—*ever* such a girl? Ah, well! when *I* was a girl—there, there—there, there!"

But before she had anything like satisfied her own query, and had got well into the room, her daughter had darted past her with a kiss that nearly upset her, laughing as she went, "Pour out my tea, mums; I'll be back in two seconds." And away she fled up the road, in a way that would have made her pupils stand aghast had they seen her. The school wicket she can manipulate in the dark with all the rapidity of long friendship, and the little aisle between the desks to the class-room door gives her even less trouble.

What her five masters thought when she followed

her short sharp knock by walking in will never be known.

What she wanted they soon knew.

"Gentlemen," she said quickly, without pause, "I understand from Mr. Bushel that you mean to give me notice of dismissal. You might have done that without allowing Mr. Bushel to insult me. I will save you the trouble by handing you my resignation *at once*. If you can get another mistress by Christmas I shall be glad, as I have the offer of a much better situation after the holidays. Good-night!"

The apparition was gone, and in its place were five dumbfounded administrators, not the least disconcerted being Bushel himself, the chairman.

For the fact is, that he thought that the magnificence of his offer had taken away the girl's breath. Of her acquiescence he never had a doubt, and he had gone back to his fellow-legislators—without revealing his real purpose—and assured them that the girl was " real downright sorry for wat 'er 'ad a done and as 'ow 'er 'oped they would look it over this time," which, in their fulness of heart, and under Bushel's influence, they had agreed to do just as the girl burst in upon them.

How they unravelled the tangle at "The Pig and Porker" need not be told. All I know is that the landlady " wondered wat 'ad a cum to 'em. 'Er 'ad never a known 'em so quiet afore in all 'er days!"

And there was further wondering elsewhere. Old Mrs. Parrington wondered at the tea-table why her daughter had rushed off so like a whirlwind. But she soon forgot that wonder in wondering whether her old lodgings at Kennington would still be open, and about them she would write this very night.

And Kate Parrington wondered, too, as to how she would get on teaching Training College students school management, for it was to her old College as a lecturer in that subject she was returning.

She wondered, too, how her successor would get on with the Bushels and Spriggses of Petti-Foggerington; and, even in the ecstasy of her newly-found joy, she found room for a big sigh for the troubles before some poor girl or other—perhaps, like herself, to come out of College to the heart-breaking toil and worry of service under the School Board for the United District of Petti-Foggerington and Great Drivellingham.

And old Mrs. Parrington wondered yet once again, some three or four hours later, to hear her daughter start from her sleep with a stifled sob.

Good soul! she put it down to the excitement of the day.

And, after all, she was right.

FADDY IN THE GIRLS' SCHOOL.

'DEAH me!" exclaims Faddy, as he enters the girls' department, screwing his eye-glass well into the corner of his eye, "some of these girls have brought their hats into school. Why is this, Miss X——? You know, they should invariably be left in the lobby."

From the character of the greeting I know that it's all U P with me—for this year, at any rate. Faddy's gout is to the fore again, or something has disagreed with him at breakfast, and lo! in the eternal fitness of things, I, the schoolmarm, must suffer. It could never occur to *his* lofty mind that careful mothers, whilst allowing their Marys and Janes to wear their best hats, being "'xamination day," would be likely to issue strict orders, with dire penalties to follow their non-fulfilment, that the said best hats must on no account be left in the lobbies. I mumble out with bated breath an abject apology respecting the hats, and go in fear and trembling for the rest of the day.

Observing that he is more than usually fretful and irascible, I move away from him, only to be called back time after time to hear in querulous tones his whining "Deah me!" The heat, the cold—the wet the dry—the light, the dark—the loud, the soft—the quick, the slow—all, all alike are wrong, irretrievably wrong, and *I* am at the bottom of it.

> His fretful temper winces at each touch,
> You always do too little or too much;
> You speak with life, in hopes to entertain,
> Your elevated voice goes through the brain;
> You fall at once into a lower key:
> That's worse—the drone-pipe of an humble-bee.
> The southern sash admits too strong a light,
> You rise and drop the curtain—*now* 'tis night.
> He shakes with cold—you stir the fire and strive
> To make a blaze—*that's* roasting him alive!

Early on in the day some class goes wrong, and Faddy waxes violent because the results do not come up to his idea of excellence! Years ago, in my innocence, I used to think that Faddy's salary, like mine, depended upon the examinations passed by the schools in his district. In this belief I forgave him when he became irritable—and even rude—to me and my pupils if they did not acquit themselves well under him. I have, of course, learned since that this is not the case, and I have tried to find some reason why Faddy should make a hard burden doubly hard to bear by losing his temper when "noughts" have to be scored instead of "passes." I am *still* trying.

I have no need to ask myself why teachers should

be similarly affected upon examination days. Faddy's inability to come anywhere near questioning in a simple, lucid, and intelligent manner has—I blush to own it—often provoked me to a forgetfulness of Dr. Watts' pious monition, "Let not your angry passions rise."

But let me not philosophise. During the morning Faddy expresses his desire, as usual, to see the exceptions: they have been standing by the while, sucking their thumbs with vacuous stare. No part of his duty gives Faddy greater delight than weighing out, probing, and testing these candidates for exemption; and it is not unusual for him to cavil and haggle for half an hour over half a dozen helpless-looking weaklings, although each of the cases has been thoroughly investigated months ago by the managers and myself.

If Faddy be unsuited for every other department of his duties, he is certainly at home among the exceptions. Fixing his glassy stare upon the first girl, he dwells long upon her perplexed countenance, as though involved in a psychological quandary, and then, turning to me, says—

"Deah me! you have her down 'Deficient in intellect'; she seems fairly intelligent. Howevah, I will question her, to see if it be as you say."

Pulling out his gold hunter, he says—

"Now, little girl, tell me, what is this?"

"A watch!" immediately retorts the deficient one.

"Deah me!" frowns Mr. Faddy, "I could not think of excusing *this* child from the examination. She is quite a sharp child—quite a sharp child!"

Seeing the look of dubiousness upon my face, he proceeds—

"Howevah, I will put anothah question to her just to convince you, Miss X——. Now, little girl, tell me, what is my watch made of?"

Without a second's consideration the weakly one blurts out—

"Brass, sir!"

Casting a look of ineffable scorn towards her, he hastily returns his watch to his fob and ejaculates with much emphasis—

"Deah me! a bad case—a very bad case. I will excuse her by all means, poor girl! Obviously deficient: I saw it at once!"

It is worthy of note that he passes the remaining exceptions without comment, and as he strikes out the names on the schedules he glances again and again with great severity at the simple one who thought his gold hunter made of brass.

Then, after spending some considerable time at my desk tying up, untying, folding, straightening out and subjecting to a variety of other processes the bundle of official papers he has brought in his bag, he turns to his assistant, who, with schedule in hand, is wearily plodding his way through an examination of half a hundred youthful readers, and says—

"What can I do, Mr. Drudge?"

"Well, sir," replies Drudge, "there are the copy-books, the needlework, and the whole of the class subjects yet untouched."

"Deah me!" sniffs Faddy, "we are getting on slowly." (Note the ingenuous implication of the *we*.) "I think I will examine the Standard I.—Recitation."

My heart is in my shoes at once, for I know of old that whenever Faddy tries his hand on the lower standards they invariably, under his experienced guidance, score a most successful failure. However, I follow him to the doomed Standard I., and he opens the ball in a quaint manner. He affects an extremely jovial attitude, "chucks" the little girls under the chin, and endearingly dubs them his "little deahs," his "duckies," and his "little wosebuds."

This familiarity, I observe with horror, is more than met half-way by the little dears in question, who become unconsciously boisterous, laugh at everything he says with charming *abandon*, and begin to look like climbing over the seats in order to fondly embrace the dear man, as all well-regulated " little duckies" naturally would do.

Just as I am determining in my own mind whether I should congratulate myself on how well things are going, or gnash my teeth with disgust at the dreadful order of the class, Faddy solves the problem by severely turning to me, and saying—

"I shall have to take serious notice in the report of the noisy and ill-behaved manner in which the children conduct themselves!"

I mentally decide "that for ways that are dark and for tricks that are mean," like the Heathen Chinee, this Inspector of schools is peculiar.

Having completely put the lower standards *hors de combat* in the recitation encounter, he sniffs the air for further conquests. "Ah, yes, the needlework! Of course, the needlework!" How shall I describe my sensations when he expresses his intention to open fire on the needlework? "I hope Drudge will take the needlework" has been my prayer for weeks; for be it known that Faddy is notorious far and wide in his district as an examiner of needlework.

At the sight of a garment "he chortles in his joy." Have you ever watched a fussy old hen amidst her newly fledged brood? If so, you have a faint presentment of Faddy among the needlework. It is just possible that when all is over, and the mistress has gone home with her heart rising within her and tears welling in her eyes, he, too, has gone his way laughing in his sleeve at the climax of absurdity which is reached when he poses as a critic of the sempstress's art. It would be far more entertaining than the most screaming farce ever penned, if it had not, alas! its serious side for the mistress.

I have got used to his fussiness, and therefore it troubles me less than it used to do, but I shall never cease to declaim against the habitual want of confidence he displays towards us. "Now, little girl, who did that corner for you?" "Did teacher fix this hem for you?" "Who finished this off for you?" "You did not make this bar yourself, did you?" Note the suggestive character of the "*for you's*" and "*did you's*" with which he turns his questions. Often and often have I heard little ones, anxious to please, *give him the answer they thought (from the form of the question) he wanted.*

"This looks as though it had been washed and ironed, Miss X——," is the only comment he makes whenever, by almost superhuman effort, I have managed to keep a piece of work free from speck or blemish.

"Ask Mr. Drudge to be so good as to take my hand-glass out of my bag" is the signal that the stitching is to be taken under review; and, with his perceptive faculties strengthened by eye and magnifying glasses, he proceeds painfully and slowly to assure himself that no more and no less than two threads have been taken up in each liliputian stitch. A similarly searching inquiry is instituted as to the composition of each of the microscopic square crosses which make up the letter-marking exercise.

It does seem absurd in these days of cheap marking-ink that valuable time, that might be spent so much more profitably and is so much needed in other directions, should be absorbed with this unprofitable ornamental marking, to say nothing of its effect upon the eyesight. "Gathering" also affords him especial delight, and magnificent are the struggles he makes to ascertain whether in every case the orthodox two threads have been religiously taken up.

Reverting to his only joy—button-holes—I think I may safely say that never have I presented a button-hole to him for inspection without the enactment of a stereotyped programme, consisting of counting to assure himself that the regulation number of stitches are in the bar and round the corner; and he never saw a seam in his life without pouncing upon it with fell intent, trying his best to tear the fabric asunder.

They tell me that specimens of work meet with

more approval from him when artistically arranged on coloured tissue paper than when presented to him in the ordinary way; but, so far, I have refused to make my school a miniature bazaar.

Perhaps lady-teachers who have a Mr. Faddy to please will note these things, and rejoice in the system that compels them to watch with anxious eyes the latest fad of their distinguished Inspector. I could tell you the secret of more than one of the few successes in Faddy's district, if it were not foreign to my weaker sex to speak uncharitably or to attribute motives.

That Faddy should have his likes and dislikes is natural enough, but it is drawing it too fine to make it a condition of goodwill that the costume shall be Puritanically plain and the hair smoothed behind the ears with Quaker-like simplicity.

But to conclude. By the time he has got through the needlework I can see the "fair" grant for sewing looming before me, because *one solitary* buttonhole has fallen off from perfection. Mr. Drudge has toiled through the rest of the work, and they depart, leaving me heartily thankful that the ordeal is over once more. I take my weary way homeward, thinking that after a year of toil it is a pity the Inspector's visit should so distress and disconcert me.

THE OLD SCHOOLMASTER'S CHRISTMAS EVE.

"Now, children, Three Cheers for the Christmas Holidays!" said the old man wearily, and with a pathetic smile that threw into dark shadow the furrows on his anxious-set face.

For one-and-forty years he had stood at that worm-eaten, rickety old desk at this time of Peace on Earth and Goodwill toward Men, and called for "Three Cheers for the Christmas Holidays!"

To-day, the second generation of those who in the old time were wont to respond with lusty throats lifted up their voices and answered with an undiminished vigour; and as the old man mutely listened, who shall say what thoughts came sadly trooping back through Memory's long avenues? Maybe he tenanted again the now cheerless bleak kitchen of the little school-house with a happy circle of faces awaiting his hand upon the latch! Maybe he heard again in Fancy's tones the gentle, loving voices silent these twenty years!

There was a whole life-time of suffering toil, softened by child-like resignation, in the old man's face while his light-hearted disciples shouted in their very fulness of joy "Hurrah!" "Hurrah!" "Hurrah!" In a moment they had mumbled after the venerable teacher—whose straggling white hairs and threadbare coat were in the strictest keeping with the poverty-stricken and age-worn character of the fabric of the village school—the Lord's Prayer, and as the dark heavy gloom and chill of the winter's night began to close around the little building and to creep in at the badly-fitting door and windows, the old man dismissed his little flock and, sinking back upon his wooden stool, folded his arms over the sloping top of his desk, and allowed his weary head to fall forward as in sleep.

"Good-bye, sir, and a merry Christmas to you, I'm sure!" respectfully curtsied the little monitress, as she timidly placed the keys upon the edge of the master's desk and stole softly away, awed that he should not have answered.

But the old pedagogue has not heard her. . . . The gloom has rolled away on either side. The old school, with its bare mildewed walls, rough uneven floor, and shambling row of desks, has given place to a modern, well-built, generously equipped institution, redolent of warmth and comfort. There are now no bickerings as to who shall manage the village school. The State has settled that long ago, and the old schoolmaster is a worthy *ex-officio* member of his District Board of Education. His views are respectfully solicited, and his opinions, being those of a ripe educationalist, are received with close attention. Not only on the platform is he the man who has voluntarily taken up a noble and exalted calling in life; and not only on the platform is he the man in whose hands, even as the clay in the hands of the potter, are the destinies of this great Umpire-State being shaped. These platitudes have come down from the platform and are walking about the village, leavening the daily treatment meted out to him.

The bitter winter night has now taken full grip of the countryside. . . . The great bell in the church tower rings out five o'clock. . . . But the gloom has rolled away on either side of the old schoolmaster, and he sleeps on. . . . The Government Inspector has just called, and the old man has conferred with him in terms of the warmest confidence and sympathy about the work of the school. Every difficulty has been generously acknowledged, and the two have concluded their fraternising by going through together some really creditable specimens of free-hand drawings of sheep, horses, cows, and the like, upon which some half-dozen of the village youngsters —about the only ones who seem to have any bent for the work—have recently been engaged.

Hark! the stroke of six tolls loud and hollow through the empty room. . . . The air is hideously cold, and the darkness has blotted out even the windows in the walls, but the gloom has rolled away from the old schoolmaster. . . . It is the day for the Local Teachers' Association to meet at his school. The members have assembled. The roll has been called, and one only, from amongst all the teachers of the district, is absent. He is ill. The front row of desks is left unfilled. Every newspaper in the county will send its representative to hear what the Teachers' Union thinks on current educational politics. For what Government could reasonably hope to stand against the united voice of the teachers of the schools of the people? And does not this Union include a membership identical—no more and no less—with the number of certificated teachers quoted in the Blue Book? Besides, according to the programme of the meeting, are not the two teacher M.P.'s to be present, and is not everyone anxious to hear what their views on the topic of the hour are?

The church clock is slowly, and with an undercurrent of wheezy cog-wheel movement, booming out "Seven!" . . . The black schoolroom is in the clutches of a clammy fog that freezes the very marrow. . . . It is appallingly silent, save where a little mouse is nibbling at a reading-book in the corner of the cupboard. But there is no longer gloom for the old schoolmaster. He sleeps on. . . . Now all is bright. For fifteen years he has sunned his declining years in the pleasant bower in front of that charming cottage nestling over beyond the Barton coppice, from which in the early summer the young wood-pigeons coo. His wife is by his side, and their two children are again playing at his feet. He has given up active school work years ago; a grateful country has generously met its obligation towards him, and has done its best to soften for him the hard track of downhill life.

Suddenly there is a sound of life in the lobby—a scraping of feet and a jarring of careless voices that break in rudely upon the silence that can be felt. The door is thrown open.

"Well, upon my word!" incisively flings out an authoritative voice. "This is a pretty state of things! I distinctly told old Wilson to be sure and have the desks put ready for the Carol Concert to-night, and he hasn't even lighted a single candle! How abominably provoking! Lydia, dear, tell him to come to me AT ONCE!"

It would have done the heart of the finest "drill" in the British Army good to have heard that "At once!" delivered.

The vicar's daughter is back in the doorway again in a breath, with the information that the little school-house is dark and empty, and that "old Wilson is nowhere to be seen."

"Abominably provoking!" bites out the vicar.

"Don't be too hard on him, pater," softly comes through the darkness. "His examination's only just over, and that's always a great worry to him, as you know."

Flash! The vicar had found his box of vestas, and a tiny glare flickers apologetically through the darkness, that seems bent on overwhelming so puny an intruder upon its domains.

"Good gracious! Whatever's the meaning of this?"

And the vicar hurries forward to where the spare

white locks of the old schoolmaster glitter back the feeble rays of the little gleam.

For a moment the stern, austere man shudders in every fibre as the extended fingers of his hand recoil from that icy touch. Then, bracing himself as with a mighty effort, he turns back through the stifling darkness—for his match has dropped from his grasp—to the doorway, where his daughter still stands.

"Lydia, my dear, run and tell Copp the blacksmith to come to me, and then go home and wait till I come. No, no, no, my darling—never mind about the concert; no questions—do as I tell you."

And Lydia wondered, as she went, at the hollow voice and chastened manner with which her father had bidden her obey him.

Selections from Cassell & Company's Publications.

Illustrated, Fine-Art, and other Volumes.

Abbeys and Churches of England and Wales, The: Descriptive, Historical, Pictorial. Series II. 21s.
Adventure, The World of. Fully Illustrated. In Three Vols. 9s. each.
Africa and its Explorers, The Story of. By Dr. ROBERT BROWN, F.L.S. Illustrated. Complete in 4 Vols., 7s. 6d. each.
Animals, Popular History of. By HENRY SCHERREN, F.Z.S. With 12 Coloured Plates and other Illustrations. 7s. 6d.
Arabian Nights Entertainments, Cassell's Pictorial. 10s. 6d.
Architectural Drawing. By R. PHENÉ SPIERS. Illustrated. 10s. 6d.
Art, The Magazine of. Yearly Vol. With 14 Photogravures or Etchings, a Series of Full-page Plates, and about 400 Illustrations. 21s.
Artistic Anatomy. By Prof. M. DUVAL. *Cheap Edition.* 3s. 6d.
Astronomy, The Dawn of. A Study of the Temple Worship and Mythology of the Ancient Egyptians. By Prof. J. NORMAN LOCKYER, C.B., F.R.S., &c. Illustrated. 21s.
Atlas, The Universal. A New and Complete General Atlas of the World, with 117 Pages of Maps, in Colours, and a Complete Index to about 125,000 Names. List of Maps, Prices and all Particulars on Application.
Bashkirtseff, Marie, The Journal of. *Cheap Edition.* 7s. 6d.
Bashkirtseff, Marie, The Letters of. 7s. 6d.
Battles of the Nineteenth Century. An Entirely New and Original Work. Illustrated. Vol. I., 9s.
Beetles, Butterflies, Moths, and Other Insects. By A. W. KAPPEL, F.E.S., and W. EGMONT KIRBY. With 12 Coloured Plates. 3s. 6d.
"Belle Sauvage" Library, The. Cloth, 2s. each. A list of the Volumes post free on application.
Biographical Dictionary, Cassell's New. *Cheap Edition*, 3s. 6d.
Birds' Nests, Eggs, and Egg-Collecting. By R. KEARTON. Illustrated with 16 Coloured Plates. 5s.
Birds' Nests, British: How, Where, and When to Find and Identify Them. By R. KEARTON. With an Introduction by Dr. BOWDLER SHARPE and upwards of 120 Illustrations of Nests, Eggs, Young, etc., from Photographs by C. KEARTON. 21s.
Breech-Loader, The, and How to Use It. By W. W. GREENER. Illustrated. New and enlarged edition. 2s. 6d.
Britain's Roll of Glory; or, the Victoria Cross, its Heroes, and their Valour. By D. H. PARRY. Illustrated. 7s. 6d.
British Ballads. With Several Hundred Original Illustrations. Complete in Two Vols., cloth, 15s. Half morocco, *price on application.*
British Battles on Land and Sea. By JAMES GRANT. With about 600 Illustrations. Four Vols., 4to, £1 16s.; *Library Edition*, £2.
Butterflies and Moths, European. With 61 Coloured Plates. 35s.
Canaries and Cage-Birds, The Illustrated Book of. With 56 Facsimile Coloured Plates, 35s. Half-morocco, £2 5s.
Captain Horn, The Adventures of. By FRANK STOCKTON. 6s.
Capture of the "Estrella," The. A Tale of the Slave Trade. By COMMANDER CLAUDE HARDING, R.N. 5s.
Cassell's Family Magazine. Yearly Vol. Illustrated. 7s. 6d.
Cathedrals, Abbeys, and Churches of England and Wales. Descriptive, Historical, Pictorial. *Popular Edition.* Two Vols. 25s.
Cats and Kittens. By HENRIETTE RONNER. With Portrait and 13 Full-page Photogravure Plates and numerous Illustrations. £2 2s.
Chums. The Illustrated Paper for Boys. Yearly Volume, 8s.
Cities of the World. Four Vols. Illustrated. 7s. 6d. each.
Civil Service, Guide to Employment in the. Entirely New Edition. Paper, 1s. Cloth, 1s. 6d.
Clinical Manuals for Practitioners and Students of Medicine. A List of Volumes forwarded post free on application to the Publishers.

5 G. 8.95

Selections from Cassell & Company's Publications.

Colour. By Prof. A. H. CHURCH. With Coloured Plates. 3s. 6d.
Commons and Forests, English. By the Rt. Hon. G. SHAW-LEFEVRE, M.P. With Maps. 10s. 6d.
Cook, The Thorough Good. By GEORGE AUGUSTUS SALA. 21s.
Cookery, A Year's. By PHYLLIS BROWNE. 3s. 6d.
Cookery Book, Cassell's New Universal. By LIZZIE HERITAGE. With 12 Coloured Plates and other Illustrations. Strongly bound in Half-leather. 1,344 pages. 6s.
Cookery, Cassell's Shilling. *110th Thousand.* 1s.
Cookery, Vegetarian. By A. G PAYNE. 1s. 6d.
Cooking by Gas, The Art of. By MARIE J. SUGG. Illustrated. 2s.
Cottage Gardening, Poultry, Bees, Allotments, Etc. Edited by W. ROBINSON. Illustrated. Half-yearly Volumes, 2s. 6d. each.
Count Cavour and Madame de Circourt. Some Unpublished Correspondence. Translated by A. J. BUTLER. Cloth gilt, 10s. 6d.
Countries of the World, The. By ROBERT BROWN, M.A., Ph.D., &c. *Cheap Edition.* Profusely Illustrated. Vol. I., 6s.
Cyclopædia, Cassell's Concise. Brought down to the latest date. With about 600 Illustrations. *Cheap Edition.* 7s. 6d.
Cyclopædia, Cassell's Miniature. Containing 30,000 subjects. Cloth, 2s. 6d.; half-roxburgh, 4s.
David Balfour, The Adventures of. By R. L. STEVENSON. Illustrated. Two Vols. 6s. each.
    Part 1.—Kidnapped.   Part 2.—Catriona.
Defoe, Daniel, The Life of. By THOMAS WRIGHT. Illustrated, 21s.
Diet and Cookery for Common Ailments. By a Fellow of the Royal College of Physicians, and PHYLLIS BROWNE. 5s.
Dog, Illustrated Book of the. By VERO SHAW, B.A. With 28 Coloured Plates. Cloth bevelled, 35s.; half-morocco, 45s.
Domestic Dictionary, The. Illustrated. Cloth, 7s. 6d.
Doré Bible, The. With 200 Full-page Illustrations by DORÉ. 15s.
Doré Don Quixote, The. With about 400 Illustrations by GUSTAVE DORÉ. *Cheap Edition.* Bevelled boards, gilt edges, 10s. 6d.
Doré Gallery, The. With 250 Illustrations by DORÉ. 4to, 42s.
Doré's Dante's Inferno. Illustrated by GUSTAVE DORÉ. With Preface by A. J. BUTLER. Cloth gilt or buckram, 7s. 6d.
Doré's Dante's Purgatory and Paradise. Illustrated by GUSTAVE DORÉ. *Cheap Edition.* 7s. 6d.
Doré's Milton's Paradise Lost. Illustrated by DORÉ. 4to, 21s. *Popular Edition.* Cloth gilt or buckram gilt, 7s. 6d.
Dorset, Old. Chapters in the History of the County. By H. J. MOULE, M.A. 10s. 6d.
Dressmaking, Modern, The Elements of. By J. E. DAVIS. Illd. 2s.
Earth, Our, and its Story. By Dr. ROBERT BROWN, F.L.S. With Coloured Plates and numerous Wood Engravings. Three Vols. 9s. each.
Edinburgh, Old and New. With 600 Illustrations. Three Vols. 9s. each.
Egypt: Descriptive, Historical, and Picturesque. By Prof. G. EBERS. With 800 Original Engravings. *Popular Edition.* In Two Vols. 42s.
Electric Current, The. How Produced and How Used. By R. MULLINEUX WALMSLEY, D.Sc., etc. Illustrated. 10s. 6d.
Electricity in the Service of Man. Illustrated. *New and Revised Edition.* 10s. 6d.
Electricity, Practical. By Prof. W. E. AYRTON. 7s. 6d.
Encyclopædic Dictionary, The. In Fourteen Divisional Vols., 10s. 6d. each; or Seven Vols., half-morocco, 21s. each; half-russia, 25s.
England, Cassell's Illustrated History of. With upwards of 2,000 Illustrations. *Revised Edition.* Complete in Eight Vols., 9s. each; cloth gilt, and embossed gilt top and headbanded, £4 net the set.

Selections from Cassell & Company's Publications.

English Dictionary, Cassell's. Giving definitions of more than 100,000 Words and Phrases. *Superior Edition*, 5s. *Cheap Edition*, 3s. 6d.
English Literature, Library of. By Prof. HENRY MORLEY. Complete in Five Vols., 7s. 6d. each.
English Literature, The Dictionary of. By W. DAVENPORT ADAMS. *Cheap Edition*, 7s. 6d.
English Literature, Morley's First Sketch of. *Revised Edition*. 7s. 6d.
English Literature, The Story of. By ANNA BUCKLAND. 3s. 6d.
English Writers. By Prof. HENRY MORLEY. Vols. I. to XI. 5s. each.
Etiquette of Good Society. *New Edition.* Edited and Revised by LADY COLIN CAMPBELL. 1s.; cloth, 1s. 6d.
Fairway Island. By HORACE HUTCHINSON. *Cheap Edition.* 3s. 6d.
Fairy Tales Far and Near. Re-told by Q. Illustrated. 3s. 6d.
Fiction, Cassell's Popular Library of. 3s. 6d. each.

THE AVENGER OF BLOOD. By J. MACLAREN COBBAN.	THE SNARE OF THE FOWLER. By Mrs. ALEXANDER.
A MODERN DICK WHITTINGTON. By JAMES PAYN.	"LA BELLA" AND OTHERS. By EGERTON CASTLE.
THE MAN IN BLACK. By STANLEY WEYMAN.	LEONA. By Mrs. MOLESWORTH.
A BLOT OF INK. Translated by Q. and PAUL M. FRANCKE.	FOURTEEN TO ONE, ETC. By ELIZABETH STUART PHELPS.
THE MEDICINE LADY. By L. T. MEADE.	FATHER STAFFORD. By ANTHONY HOPE.
OUT OF THE JAWS OF DEATH. By FRANK BARRETT.	DR. DUMÁNY'S WIFE. By MAURUS JÓKAI.
	THE DOINGS OF RAFFLES HAW. By CONAN DOYLE.

Field Naturalist's Handbook, The. By the Revs. J. G. WOOD and THEODORE WOOD. *Cheap Edition.* 2s. 6d.
Figuier's Popular Scientific Works. With Several Hundred Illustrations in each. Newly Revised and Corrected. 3s. 6d. each.
  THE HUMAN RACE.   MAMMALIA.   OCEAN WORLD.
    THE INSECT WORLD.   REPTILES AND BIRDS.
  WORLD BEFORE THE DELUGE.   THE VEGETABLE WORLD.
Flora's Feast. A Masque of Flowers. Penned and Pictured by WALTER CRANE. With 40 Pages in Colours. 5s.
Football, The Rugby Union Game. Edited by REV. F. MARSHALL. Illustrated. *New and Enlarged Edition.* 7s. 6d.
For Glory and Renown. By D. H. PARRY. Illustrated. 5s.
France, From the Memoirs of a Minister of. By STANLEY WEYMAN. 6s.
Franco-German War, Cassell's History of the. Complete in Two Vols. Containing about 500 Illustrations. 9s. each.
Free Lance in a Far Land, A. By HERBERT COMPTON. 6s.
Garden Flowers, Familiar. By SHIRLEY HIBBERD. With Coloured Plates by F. E. HULME, F.L.S. Complete in Five Series. 12s. 6d. each.
Gardening, Cassell's Popular. Illustrated. Four Vols. 5s. each.
Gazetteer of Great Britain and Ireland, Cassell's. Illustrated. Vols. I. and II. 7s. 6d. each.
Gladstone, William Ewart, The People's Life of. Illustrated. 1s.
Gleanings from Popular Authors. Two Vols. With Original Illustrations 4to, 9s. each. Two Vols. in One, 15s.
Gulliver's Travels. With 88 Engravings by MORTEN. *Cheap Edition.* Cloth, 3s. 6d.; cloth gilt, 5s.
Gun and its Development, The. By W. W. GREENER. With 500 Illustrations. 10s. 6d.
Heavens, The Story of the. By Sir ROBERT STAWELL BALL, LL.D., F.R.S., F.R.A.S. With Coloured Plates. *Popular Edition.* 12s. 6d.
Heroes of Britain in Peace and War. With 300 Original Illustrations. Two Vols., 3s. 6d. each; or One Vol., 7s. 6d.
Highway of Sorrow, The. By HESBA STRETTON and ********. 6s.

Selections from Cassell & Company's Publications.

Hispaniola Plate (1683-1893). By JOHN BLOUNDELLE-BURTON. 6s.
Historic Houses of the United Kingdom. Profusely Illustrated. 10s. 6d.
History, A Foot-note to. Eight Years of Trouble in Samoa. By ROBERT LOUIS STEVENSON. 6s.
Home Life of the Ancient Greeks, The. Translated by ALICE ZIMMERN. Illustrated. *Cheap Edition.* 5s.
Horse, The Book of the. By SAMUEL SIDNEY. With 17 Full-page Collotype Plates of Celebrated Horses of the Day, and numerous other Illustrations. Cloth, 15s.
Horses and Dogs. By O. EERELMAN. With Descriptive Text. Translated from the Dutch by CLARA BELL. With Photogravure Frontispiece, 12 Exquisite Collotypes, and several full page and other engravings in the text. 25s. net.
Houghton, Lord: The Life, Letters, and Friendships of Richard Monckton Milnes, First Lord Houghton. By Sir WEMYSS REID. In Two Vols., with Two Portraits. 32s.
Household, Cassell's Book of the. Complete in Four Vols. 5s. each. Four Vols. in Two, half-morocco, 25s.
Hygiene and Public Health. By B. ARTHUR WHITELEGGE, M.D. 7s. 6d.
Impregnable City, The. By MAX PEMBERTON. 6s.
India, Cassell's History of. By JAMES GRANT. With about 400 Illustrations. Two Vols., 9s. each. One Vol., 15s.
Iron Pirate, The. By MAX PEMBERTON. Illustrated. 5s.
Island Nights' Entertainments. By R. L. STEVENSON. Illustrated. 6s.
Kennel Guide, The Practical. By Dr. GORDON STABLES. 1s.
Khiva, A Ride to. By Col. FRED BURNABY. *New Edition.* With Portrait and Seven Illustrations. 3s. 6d.
King George, In the Days of. By COL. PERCY GROVES. Illd. 1s. 6d.
King's Hussar, A. Edited by HERBERT COMPTON. 6s.
Ladies' Physician, The. By a London Physician. *Cheap Edition Revised and Enlarged.* 3s. 6d.
Lady Biddy Fane, The Admirable. By FRANK BARRETT. *New Edition.* With 12 Full-page Illustrations. 6s.
Lady's Dressing-room, The. Translated from the French of BARONESS STAFFE by LADY COLIN CAMPBELL. 3s. 6d.
Letters, the Highway of, and its Echoes of Famous Footsteps. By THOMAS ARCHER. Illustrated. 10s. 6d.
Letts's Diaries and other Time-saving Publications published exclusively by CASSELL & COMPANY. (*A list free on application.*)
'Lisbeth. A Novel. By LESLIE KEITH. 6s.
List, ye Landsmen! By W. CLARK RUSSELL. 6s.
Little Minister, The. By J. M. BARRIE. *Illustrated Edition.* 6s.
Little Squire, The. By Mrs. HENRY DE LA PASTURE. 3s. 6d.
Llollandllaff Legends, The. By LOUIS LLOLLANDLLAFF. 1s.; cloth, 2s.
Lobengula, Three Years With, and Experiences in South Africa. By J. COOPER-CHADWICK. *Cheap Edition,* 2s. 6d.
Locomotive Engine, The Biography of a. By HENRY FRITH. 3s. 6d.
Loftus, Lord Augustus, The Diplomatic Reminiscences of. First and Second Series. Two Vols., each with Portrait, 32s. each Series.
London, Greater. By EDWARD WALFORD. Two Vols. With about 400 Illustrations. 9s. each.
London, Old and New. Six Vols., each containing about 200 Illustrations and Maps. Cloth, 9s. each.
Lost on Du Corrig; or, 'Twixt Earth and Ocean. By STANDISH O'GRADY. With 8 Full-page Illustrations. 5s.
Medicine, Manuals for Students of. (*A List forwarded post free.*)
Modern Europe, A History of. By C. A. FYFFE, M.A. *Cheap Edition in One Volume,* 10s. 6d. Library Edition. Illustrated. 3 Vols., 7s. 6d. each.
Mount Desolation. An Australian Romance. By W. CARLTON DAWE. *Cheap Edition.* 3s. 6d.

Selections from Cassell & Company's Publications.

Music, Illustrated History of. By EMIL NAUMANN. Edited by the Rev. Sir F. A. GORE OUSELEY, Bart. Illustrated. Two Vols. 31s. 6d.

National Library, Cassell's. In 214 Volumes. Paper covers, 3d.; cloth, 6d. (*A Complete List of the Volumes post free on application.*)

Natural History, Cassell's Concise. By E. PERCEVAL WRIGHT, M.A., M.D., F.L.S. With several Hundred Illustrations. 7s. 6d.

Natural History, Cassell's New. Edited by Prof. P. MARTIN DUNCAN, M.B., F.R.S., F.G.S. Complete in Six Vols. With about 2,000 Illustrations. Cloth, 9s. each.

Nature's Wonder Workers. By KATE R. LOVELL. Illustrated. 3s. 6d.

New England Boyhood, A. By EDWARD E. HALE. 3s. 6d.

New Zealand, Picturesque. With Preface by Sir W. B. PERCEVAL, K.C.M.G. Illustrated. 6s.

Nursing for the Home and for the Hospital, A Handbook of. By CATHERINE J. WOOD. *Cheap Edition.* 1s. 6d.; cloth, 2s.

Nursing of Sick Children, A Handbook for the. By CATHERINE J. WOOD. 2s. 6d.

Ohio, The New. A Story of East and West. By EDWARD E. HALE. 6s.

Oil Painting, A Manual of. By the Hon. JOHN COLLIER. 2s. 6d.

Old Maids and Young. By E. D'ESTERRE KEELING. 6s.

Old Boy's Yarns, An. By HAROLD AVERY. With 8 Plates. 3s. 6d.

Our Own Country. Six Vols. With 1,200 Illustrations. 7s. 6d. each.

Painting, The English School of. *Cheap Edition.* 3s. 6d.

Painting, Practical Guides to. With Coloured Plates:—

MARINE PAINTING. 5s.	WATER-COLOUR PAINTING. 5s.
ANIMAL PAINTING. 5s.	NEUTRAL TINT. 5s.
CHINA PAINTING. 5s.	SEPIA, in Two Vols., 3s. each; or in One Vol., 5s.
FIGURE PAINTING. 7s. 6d.	
ELEMENTARY FLOWER PAINTING. 3s.	FLOWERS, AND HOW TO PAINT THEM. 5s.

Paris, Old and New. A Narrative of its History, its People, and its Places. By H. SUTHERLAND EDWARDS. Profusely Illustrated. Complete in Two Vols., 9s. each; or gilt edges, 10s. 6d. each.

Peoples of the World, The. In Six Vols. By Dr. ROBERT BROWN. Illustrated. 7s. 6d. each.

Photography for Amateurs. By T. C. HEPWORTH. *Enlarged and Revised Edition.* Illustrated. 1s.; or cloth, 1s. 6d.

Phrase and Fable, Dr. Brewer's Dictionary of. Giving the Derivation, Source, or Origin of Common Phrases, Allusions, and Words that have a Tale to Tell. *Entirely New and Greatly Enlarged Edition.* 10s. 6d.

Picturesque America. Complete in Four Vols., with 48 Exquisite Steel Plates and about 800 Original Wood Engravings. £2 2s. each. *Popular Edition*, Vols. I. & II., 18s. each. [the Set.

Picturesque Canada. With 600 Original Illustrations. Two Vols. £6 6s.

Picturesque Europe. Complete in Five Vols. Each containing 13 Exquisite Steel Plates, from Original Drawings, and nearly 200 Original Illustrations. Cloth, £21; half-morocco, £31 10s.; morocco gilt, £52 10s. POPULAR EDITION. In Five Vols., 18s. each.

Picturesque Mediterranean, The. With Magnificent Original Illustrations by the leading Artists of the Day. Complete in Two Vols. £2 2s. each.

Pigeon Keeper, The Practical. By LEWIS WRIGHT. Illustrated. 3s. 6d.

Pigeons, Fulton's Book of. Edited by LEWIS WRIGHT. Revised, Enlarged and supplemented by the Rev. W. F. LUMLEY. With 50 Full-page Illustrations. *Popular Edition.* In One Vol., 10s. 6d.

Planet, The Story of Our. By T. G. BONNEY, D.Sc., LL.D., F.R.S., F.S.A., F.G.S. With Coloured Plates and Maps and about 100 Illustrations. 31s. 6d.

Pocket Library, Cassell's. Cloth, 1s. 4d. each.
    A King's Diary. By PERCY WHITE.
    A White Baby. By JAMES WELSH.
    The Little Huguenot. By MAX PEMBERTON.
    A Whirl Asunder. By GERTRUDE ATHERTON.

Selections from Cassell & Company's Publications.

Poems, Aubrey de Vere's. A Selection. Edited by J. DENNIS. 3s. 6d.
Poets, Cassell's Miniature Library of the. Price 1s. each Vol.
Pomona's Travels. By FRANK R. STOCKTON. Illustrated. 5s.
Portrait Gallery, The Cabinet. Complete in Five Series, each containing 36 Cabinet Photographs of Eminent Men and Women. 15s. each.
Portrait Gallery, Cassell's Universal. Containing 240 Portraits of Celebrated Men and Women of the Day. With brief Memoirs and *facsimile* Autographs. Cloth, 6s.
Poultry Keeper, The Practical. By L. WRIGHT. Illustrated. 3s. 6d.
Poultry, The Book of. By LEWIS WRIGHT. *Popular Edition.* 10s. 6d.
Poultry, The Illustrated Book of. By LEWIS WRIGHT. With Fifty Coloured Plates. *New and Revised Edition.* Cloth, gilt edges (*Price on application*). Half-morocco, £2 2s.
Prison Princess, A. By Major ARTHUR GRIFFITHS. 6s.
"Punch," The History of. By M. H. SPIELMANN. With upwards of 160 Illustrations, Portraits, and Facsimiles. Cloth, 16s.; *Large Paper Edition*, £2 2s. net.
Q's Works, Uniform Edition of. 5s. each.

Dead Man's Rock.	The Astonishing History of Troy Town.
The Splendid Spur.	"I Saw Three Ships," and other Winter's Tales.
The Blue Pavilions.	Noughts and Crosses.
The Delectable Duchy.	

Queen Summer; or, The Tourney of the Lily and the Rose. With Forty Pages of Designs in Colours by WALTER CRANE. 6s.
Queen, The People's Life of their. By Rev. E. J HARDY, M.A. 1s.
Queen Victoria, The Life and Times of. By ROBERT WILSON. Complete in Two Vols. With numerous Illustrations. 9s. each.
Queen's Scarlet, The. By G. MANVILLE FENN. Illustrated. 5s.
Rabbit-Keeper, The Practical. By CUNICULUS. Illustrated. 3s. 6d.
Railways, Our. Their Origin, Development, Incident, and Romance. By JOHN PENDLETON. Illustrated. 2 Vols., 24s.
Railway Guides, Official Illustrated. With Illustrations, Maps, &c. Price 1s. each; or in cloth, 2s. each.

LONDON AND NORTH WESTERN RAILWAY.	GREAT EASTERN RAILWAY.
GREAT WESTERN RAILWAY.	LONDON AND SOUTH WESTERN RAILWAY.
MIDLAND RAILWAY.	LONDON, BRIGHTON AND SOUTH COAST RAILWAY.
GREAT NORTHERN RAILWAY.	SOUTH-EASTERN RAILWAY.

Railway Guides, Official Illustrated. Abridged and Popular Editions. Paper covers, 3d. each.

GREAT EASTERN RAILWAY.	LONDON AND SOUTH WESTERN RAILWAY.
LONDON AND NORTH WESTERN RAILWAY.	

Railway Library, Cassell's. Crown 8vo, boards, 2s. each. (*A List of the Vols. post free on application.*)
Red Terror, The. A Story of the Paris Commune. By EDWARD KING. Illustrated. 3s. 6d.
Rivers of Great Britain: Descriptive, Historical, Pictorial.
 THE ROYAL RIVER: The Thames, from Source to Sea. 16s.
 RIVERS OF THE EAST COAST. *Popular Edition*, 16s.
Robinson Crusoe, Cassell's New Fine-Art Edition of. 7s. 6d.
Romance, The World of. Illustrated. Cloth, 9s.
Royal Academy Pictures, 1895. With upwards of 200 magnificent reproductions of Pictures in the Royal Academy of 1895. 7s. 6d.
Russo-Turkish War, Cassell's History of. With about 500 Illustrations. Two Vols. 9s. each.
Sala, George Augustus, The Life and Adventures of. By Himself. In Two Vols., demy 8vo, cloth, 32s.
Saturday Journal, Cassell's. Yearly Volume, cloth, 7s. 6d.

Selections from Cassell & Company's Publications.

Science Series, The Century. Consisting of Biographies of Eminent Scientific Men of the present Century. Edited by Sir HENRY ROSCOE, D.C.L., F.R.S. Crown 8vo, 3s. 6d. each.
 John Dalton and the Rise of Modern Chemistry. By Sir HENRY E. ROSCOE, F.R.S.
 Major Rennell, F.R.S., and the Rise of English Geography. By CLEMENTS R. MARKHAM, C.B., F.R.S., President of the Royal Geographical Society.
 Justus Von Liebig: His Life and Work. By W. A. SHENSTONE, F.I.C.
 The Herschels and Modern Astronomy. By MISS AGNES M. CLERKE.
 Charles Lyell: His Life and Work. By Professor T. G. BONNEY, F.R.S.

Science for All. Edited by Dr. ROBERT BROWN. Five Vols. 9s. each.

Scotland, Picturesque and Traditional. A Pilgrimage with Staff and Knapsack. By G. E. EYRE-TODD. 6s.

Sea, The Story of the. An Entirely New and Original Work. Edited by Q. Illustrated. Vol. I. 9s.

Sea Wolves, The. By MAX PEMBERTON. Illustrated. 6s.

Shadow of a Song The. A Novel. By CECIL HARLEY. 5s.

Shaftesbury, The Seventh Earl of, K.G., The Life and Work of. By EDWIN HODDER. *Cheap Edition.* 3s. 6d.

Shakespeare, The Plays of. Edited by Professor HENRY MORLEY. Complete in Thirteen Vols., cloth, 21s.; half-morocco, cloth sides, 42s.

Shakespeare, Cassell's Quarto Edition. Containing about 600 Illustrations by H. C. SELOUS. Complete in Three Vols., cloth gilt, £3 3s.

Shakespeare, The England of. *New Edition.* By E. GOADBY. With Full-page Illustrations. 2s. 6d.

Shakspere's Works. *Édition de Luxe.*
 "King Henry VIII." Illustrated by SIR JAMES LINTON, P.R.I. (*Price on application.*)
 "Othello." Illustrated by FRANK DICKSEE, R.A. £3 10s.
 "King Henry IV." Illustrated by EDUARD GRÜTZNER. £3 10s.
 "As You Like It." Illustrated by ÉMILE BAYARD. £3 10s.

Shakspere, The Leopold. With 400 Illustrations. *Cheap Edition.* 3s. 6d. Cloth gilt, gilt edges, 5s.; Roxburgh, 7s. 6d.

Shakspere, The Royal. With Steel Plates and Wood Engravings. Three Vols. 15s. each.

Sketches, The Art of Making and Using. From the French of G. FRAIPONT. By CLARA BELL. With 50 Illustrations. 2s. 6d.

Smuggling Days and Smuggling Ways. By Commander the Hon. HENRY N. SHORE, R.N. With numerous Illustrations. 7s. 6d.

Social England. A Record of the Progress of the People. By various writers. Edited by H. D. TRAILL, D.C.L. Vols. I., II., & III., 15s. each. Vol. IV., 17s.

Social Welfare, Subjects of. By Rt. Hon. LORD PLAYFAIR, K.C.B. 7s. 6d.

Sports and Pastimes, Cassell's Complete Book of. *Cheap Edition.* With more than 900 Illustrations. Medium 8vo, 992 pages, cloth, 3s. 6d.

Squire, The. By Mrs. PARR. *Popular Edition.* 6s.

Standishs of High Acre, The. A Novel. By GILBERT SHELDON. Two Vols. 21s.

Star-Land. By Sir R. S. BALL, LL.D., &c. Illustrated. 6s.

Statesmen, Past and Future. 6s.

Story of Francis Cludde, The. By STANLEY J. WEYMAN. 6s.

Story Poems. For Young and Old. Edited by E. DAVENPORT. 3s. 6d.

Sun, The. By Sir ROBERT STAWELL BALL, LL.D., F.R.S., F.R.A.S. With Eight Coloured Plates and other Illustrations. 21s.

Sunshine Series, Cassell's. 1s. each.
 (*A List of the Volumes post free on application.*)

Thackeray in America, With. By EYRE CROWE, A.R.A. Ill. 10s. 6d.

The "Treasure Island" Series. *Illustrated Edition.* 3s. 6d. each.

Treasure Island. By ROBERT LOUIS STEVENSON.	**The Black Arrow.** By ROBERT LOUIS STEVENSON.
The Master of Ballantrae. By ROBERT LOUIS STEVENSON.	**King Solomon's Mines.** By H. RIDER HAGGARD.

Selections from Cassell & Company's Publications.

Things I have Seen and People I have Known. By G. A. SALA. With Portrait and Autograph. 2 Vols. 21s.

Tidal Thames, The. By GRANT ALLEN. With India Proof Impressions of Twenty magnificent Full-page Photogravure Plates, and with many other Illustrations in the Text after Original Drawings by W. L. WYLLIE, A.R.A. Half morocco. £5 15s. 6d.

Tiny Luttrell. By E. W. HORNUNG. *Popular Edition.* 6s.

To Punish the Czar: a Story of the Crimea. By HORACE HUTCHINSON. Illustrated. 3s. 6d.

Treatment, The Year-Book of, for 1896. A Critical Review for Practitioners of Medicine and Surgery. *Twelfth Year of Issue.* 7s. 6d.

Trees, Familiar. By G. S. BOULGER, F.L.S. Two Series. With 40 full-page Coloured Plates by W. H. J. BOOT. 12s. 6d. each.

Tuxter's Little Maid. By G. B. BURGIN. 6s.

"Unicode": the Universal Telegraphic Phrase Book. *Desk or Pocket Edition.* 2s. 6d.

United States, Cassell's History of the. By EDMUND OLLIER. With 600 Illustrations. Three Vols. 9s. each.

Universal History, Cassell's Illustrated. Four Vols. 9s. each.

Vision of Saints, A. By Sir LEWIS MORRIS. With 20 Full-page Illustrations. Crown 4to, cloth, 10s. 6d. *Non-illustrated Edition*, 6s.

Wandering Heath. Short Stories. By Q. 6s.

War and Peace, Memories and Studies of. By ARCHIBALD FORBES. 16s.

Westminster Abbey, Annals of. By E. T. BRADLEY (Mrs. A. MURRAY SMITH). Illustrated. With a Preface by Dean BRADLEY. 63s.

White Shield, The. By BERTRAM MITFORD. 6s.

Wild Birds, Familiar. By W. SWAYSLAND. Four Series. With 40 Coloured Plates in each. (Sold in sets only; price on application.)

Wild Flowers, Familiar. By F. E. HULME, F.L.S., F.S.A. Five Series. With 40 Coloured Plates in each. (In sets only; price on application.)

Wild Flowers Collecting Book. In Six Parts, 4d. each.

Wild Flowers Drawing and Painting Book. In Six Parts, 4d. each.

Windsor Castle, The Governor's Guide to. By the Most Noble the MARQUIS OF LORNE, K.T. Profusely Illustrated. Limp Cloth, 1s. Cloth boards, gilt edges, 2s.

Wit and Humour, Cassell's New World of. With New Pictures and New Text. 6s.

With Claymore and Bayonet. By Col. PERCY GROVES. Illd. 5s.

Wood, Rev. J. G., Life of the. By the Rev. THEODORE WOOD. Extra crown 8vo, cloth. *Cheap Edition.* 3s. 6d.

Work. The Illustrated Weekly Journal for Mechanics. Vol. IX., 4s.

"Work" Handbooks. Practical Manuals prepared *under the direction of* PAUL N. HASLUCK, Editor of *Work*. Illustrated. 1s. each.

World Beneath the Waters, A. By Rev. GERARD BANCKS. 3s. 6d.

World of Wonders. Two Vols. With 400 Illustrations. 7s. 6d. each.

Wrecker, The. By R. L. STEVENSON and L. OSBOURNE. Illustrated. 6s.

Yule Tide. Cassell's Christmas Annual. 1s.

ILLUSTRATED MAGAZINES.

The Quiver. Monthly, 6d.

Cassell's Family Magazine. Monthly, 6d.

"Little Folks" Magazine. Monthly, 6d.

The Magazine of Art. Monthly, 1s. 4d.

"Chums." Illustrated Paper for Boys. Weekly, 1d.; Monthly, 6d.

Cassell's Saturday Journal. Weekly, 1d.; Monthly, 6d.

Work. Weekly, 1d.; Monthly, 6d.

Cottage Gardening. Weekly, ½d.; Monthly, 3d.

CASSELL & COMPANY, LIMITED, *Ludgate Hill, London.*

Selections from Cassell & Company's Publications.

Bibles and Religious Works.

Bible Biographies. Illustrated. 2s. 6d. each.
    The Story of Moses and Joshua. By the Rev. J. TELFORD.
    The Story of the Judges. By the Rev. J. WYCLIFFE GEDGE.
    The Story of Samuel and Saul. By the Rev. D. C. TOVEY
    The Story of David. By the Rev. J. WILD.
    The Story of Joseph. Its Lessons for To-Day. By the Rev. GEORGE BAINTON.
    The Story of Jesus. In Verse. By J. R. MACDUFF, D.D.

Bible, Cassell's Illustrated Family. With 900 Illustrations. Leather, gilt edges, £2 10s.
Bible Educator, The. Edited by the Very Rev. Dean PLUMPTRE, D.D. With Illustrations, Maps, &c. Four Vols., cloth, 6s. each.
Bible Manual, Cassell's Illustrated. By the Rev. ROBERT HUNTER, LL.D. *Illustrated.* 7s. 6d.
Bible Student in the British Museum, The. By the Rev. J. G. KITCHIN, M.A. *New and Revised Edition.* 1s. 4d.
Biblewomen and Nurses. Yearly Volume. Illustrated. 3s.
Bunyan, Cassell's Illustrated. With 200 Original Illustrations. *Cheap Edition.* 7s. 6d.
Bunyan's Pilgrim's Progress. Illustrated throughout. Cloth, 3s. 6d.; cloth gilt, gilt edges, 5s.
Child's Bible, The. With 200 Illustrations. *150th Thousand.* 7s. 6d.
Child's Life of Christ, The. With 200 Illustrations. 7s. 6d.
"Come, ye Children." Illustrated. By Rev. BENJAMIN WAUGH. 3s. 6d.
Conquests of the Cross. Illustrated. In 3 Vols. 9s. each.
Doré Bible. With 238 Illustrations by GUSTAVE DORÉ. Small folio, best morocco, gilt edges, £15. *Popular Edition.* With 200 Illustrations. 15s.
Early Days of Christianity, The. By the Very Rev. Dean FARRAR, D.D., F.R.S. LIBRARY EDITION. Two Vols., 24s.; morocco, £2 2s. POPULAR EDITION. Complete in One Volume, cloth, 6s.; cloth, gilt edges, 7s. 6d.; Persian morocco, 10s. 6d.; tree-calf, 15s.
Family Prayer-Book, The. Edited by Rev. Canon GARBETT, M.A., and Rev. S. MARTIN. With Full page Illustrations. *New Edition.* Cloth, 7s. 6d.
Gleanings after Harvest. Studies and Sketches by the Rev. JOHN R. VERNON, M.A. Illustrated. 6s.
"Graven in the Rock." By the Rev. Dr. SAMUEL KINNS, F.R.A.S., Author of "Moses and Geology." Illustrated. 12s. 6d.
"Heart Chords." A Series of Works by Eminent Divines. Bound in cloth, red edges, One Shilling each.

MY BIBLE. By the Right Rev. W. BOYD CARPENTER, Bishop of Ripon.
MY FATHER. By the Right Rev. ASHTON OXENDEN, late Bishop of Montreal.
MY WORK FOR GOD. By the Right Rev. Bishop COTTERILL.
MY OBJECT IN LIFE. By the Very Rev. Dean FARRAR, D.D.
MY ASPIRATIONS. By the Rev. G. MATHESON, D.D.
MY EMOTIONAL LIFE. By the Rev. Preb. CHADWICK, D.D.
MY BODY. By the Rev. Prof. W. G. BLAIKIE, D.D.
MY GROWTH IN DIVINE LIFE. By the Rev. Preb. REYNOLDS, M.A.
MY SOUL. By the Rev. P. B. POWER, M.A.
MY HEREAFTER. By the Very Rev. Dean BICKERSTETH.
MY WALK WITH GOD. By the Very Rev. Dean MONTGOMERY.
MY AIDS TO THE DIVINE LIFE. By the Very Rev. Dean BOYLE.
MY SOURCES OF STRENGTH. By the Rev. E. E. JENKINS, M.A., Secretary of Wesleyan Missionary Society.

Helps to Belief. A Series of Helpful Manuals on the Religious Difficulties of the Day. Edited by the Rev. TEIGNMOUTH SHORE, M.A., Canon of Worcester. Cloth, 1s. each.

CREATION. By Harvey Goodwin, D.D., late Bishop of Carlisle.
THE DIVINITY OF OUR LORD. By the Lord Bishop of Derry.
MIRACLES. By the Rev. Brownlow Maitland, M.A.
PRAYER. By the Rev. Canon Shore, M.A.
THE ATONEMENT. By William Connor Magee, D.D., Late Archbishop of York.

5 B. 8.95

Selections from Cassell & Company's Publications.

Holy Land and the Bible, The. By the Rev. C. Geikie, D.D., LL.D. (Edin.). Two Vols., 24s. *Illustrated Edition,* One Vol., 21s.

Life of Christ, The. By the Very Rev. Dean Farrar, D.D., F.R.S. Library Edition. Two Vols. Cloth, 24s.; morocco, 42s. Cheap Illustrated Edition. Cloth, 7s. 6d.; cloth, full gilt, gilt edges, 10s. 6d. Popular Edition (*Revised and Enlarged*), 8vo, cloth, gilt edges, 7s. 6d.; Persian morocco, gilt edges, 10s. 6d.; tree-calf, 15s.

Moses and Geology; or, The Harmony of the Bible with Science. By the Rev. Samuel Kinns, Ph.D., F.R.A.S. Illustrated. *New Edition.* 10s. 6d.

My Last Will and Testament. By Hyacinthe Loyson (Père Hyacinthe). Translated by Fabian Ware. 1s.; cloth, 1s. 6d.

New Light on the Bible and the Holy Land. By B. T. A. Evetts, M.A. Illustrated. 21s.

New Testament Commentary for English Readers, The. Edited by Bishop Ellicott. In Three Volumes. 21s. each. Vol. I.—The Four Gospels. Vol. II.—The Acts, Romans, Corinthians, Galatians. Vol. III.—The remaining Books of the New Testament.

New Testament Commentary. Edited by Bishop Ellicott. Handy Volume Edition. St. Matthew, 3s. 6d. St. Mark, 3s. St. Luke, 3s. 6d. St. John, 3s. 6d. The Acts of the Apostles, 3s. 6d. Romans, 2s. 6d. Corinthians I. and II., 3s. Galatians, Ephesians, and Philippians, 3s. Colossians, Thessalonians, and Timothy, 3s. Titus, Philemon, Hebrews, and James, 3s. Peter, Jude, and John, 3s. The Revelation, 3s. An Introduction to the New Testament, 3s. 6d.

Old Testament Commentary for English Readers, The. Edited by Bishop Ellicott. Complete in Five Vols. 21s. each. Vol. I.—Genesis to Numbers. Vol. II.—Deuteronomy to Samuel II. Vol. III.—Kings I. to Esther. Vol. IV.—Job to Isaiah. Vol. V.—Jeremiah to Malachi.

Old Testament Commentary. Edited by Bishop Ellicott. Handy Volume Edition. Genesis, 3s. 6d. Exodus, 3s. Leviticus, 3s. Numbers, 2s. 6d. Deuteronomy, 2s. 6d.

Plain Introductions to the Books of the Old Testament. Edited by Bishop Ellicott. 3s. 6d.

Plain Introductions to the Books of the New Testament. Edited by Bishop Ellicott. 3s. 6d.

Protestantism, The History of. By the Rev. J. A. Wylie, LL.D. Containing upwards of 600 Original Illustrations. Three Vols. 9s. each.

Quiver Yearly Volume, The. With about 600 Original Illustrations. 7s. 6d.

Religion, The Dictionary of. By the Rev. W. Benham, B.D. *Cheap Edition.* 10s. 6d.

St. George for England; and other Sermons preached to Children. By the Rev. T. Teignmouth Shore, M.A., Canon of Worcester. 5s.

St. Paul, The Life and Work of. By the Very Rev. Dean Farrar, D.D., F.R.S. Library Edition. Two Vols., cloth, 24s.; calf, 42s. Illustrated Edition, complete in One Volume, with about 300 Illustrations, £1 1s.; morocco, £2 2s. Popular Edition. One Volume, 8vo, cloth, 6s.; cloth, gilt edges, 7s. 6d.; Persian morocco, 10s. 6d.; tree-calf, 15s.

Shall We Know One Another in Heaven? By the Rt. Rev. J. C. Ryle, D.D., Bishop of Liverpool. *Cheap Edition.* Paper covers, 6d.

Searchings in the Silence. By Rev. George Matheson, D.D. 3s. 6d.

"Sunday," Its Origin, History, and Present Obligation. By the Ven. Archdeacon Hessey, D.C.L. *Fifth Edition.* 7s. 6d.

Twilight of Life, The. Words of Counsel and Comfort for the Aged. By the Rev. John Ellerton, M.A. 1s. 6d.

Selections from Cassell & Company's Publications.

Educational Works and Students' Manuals.

Agricultural Text-Books, Cassell's. (The "Downton" Series.) Edited by JOHN WRIGHTSON, Professor of Agriculture. Fully Illustrated, 2s. 6d. each.—Farm Crops. By Prof. WRIGHTSON.—Soils and Manures. By J. M. H. MUNRO, D.Sc. (London), F.I.C., F.C.S.—Live Stock. By Prof. WRIGHTSON.

Alphabet, Cassell's Pictorial. 3s. 6d.

Arithmetics, Cassell's "Belle Sauvage." By GEORGE RICKS, B.Sc. Lond. With Test Cards. (*List on application.*)

Atlas, Cassell's Popular. Containing 24 Coloured Maps. 2s. 6d.

Book-Keeping. By THEODORE JONES. For Schools, 2s.; cloth, 3s. For the Million, 2s.; cloth, 3s. Books for Jones's System, 2s.

British Empire Map of the World. By G. R. PARKIN and J. G. BARTHOLOMEW, F.R.G.S. 25s.

Chemistry, The Public School. By J. H. ANDERSON, M.A. 2s. 6d.

Cookery for Schools. By LIZZIE HERITAGE. 6d.

Dulce Domum. Rhymes and Songs for Children. Edited by JOHN FARMER, Editor of "Gaudeamus," &c. Old Notation and Words, 5s. N.B.—The words of the Songs in "Dulce Domum" (with the Airs both in Tonic Sol-fa and Old Notation) can be had in Two Parts, 6d. each.

Euclid, Cassell's. Edited by Prof. WALLACE, M.A. 1s.

Euclid, The First Four Books of. *New Edition.* In paper, 6d.; cloth, 9d.

Experimental Geometry. By PAUL BERT. Illustrated. 1s. 6d.

French, Cassell's Lessons in. *New and Revised Edition.* Parts I. and II., each 2s. 6d.; complete, 4s. 6d. Key, 1s. 6d.

French-English and English-French Dictionary. *Entirely New and Enlarged Edition.* Cloth, 3s. 6d.; superior binding, 5s.

French Reader, Cassell's Public School. By G. S. CONRAD. 2s. 6d.

Gaudeamus. Songs for Colleges and Schools. Edited by JOHN FARMER. 5s. Words only, paper covers, 6d.; cloth, 9d.

German Dictionary, Cassell's New (German-English, English-German). *Cheap Edition.* Cloth, 3s. 6d. *Superior Binding*, 5s.

Hand and Eye Training. By G. RICKS, B.Sc. 2 Vols., with 16 Coloured Plates in each Vol. Cr. 4to, 6s. each. Cards for Class Use, 5 sets, 1s. each.

Hand and Eye Training. By GEORGE RICKS, B.Sc., and JOSEPH VAUGHAN. Illustrated. Vol. I. Designing with Coloured Papers. Vol. II. Cardboard Work. 2s. each. Vol. III. Colour Work and Design, 3s.

Historical Cartoons, Cassell's Coloured. Size 45 in. × 35 in., 2s. each. Mounted on canvas and varnished, with rollers, 5s. each.

Italian Lessons, with Exercises, Cassell's. Cloth, 3s. 6d.

Latin Dictionary, Cassell's New. (Latin-English and English-Latin.) Revised by J. R. V. MARCHANT, M.A., and J. F. CHARLES, B.A. Cloth, 3s. 6d. *Superior Binding*, 5s.

Latin Primer, The First. By Prof. POSTGATE. 1s.

Latin Primer, The New. By Prof. J. P. POSTGATE. 2s. 6d.

Latin Prose for Lower Forms. By M. A. BAYFIELD, M.A. 2s. 6d.

Laws of Every-Day Life. By H. O. ARNOLD-FORSTER, M.P. 1s. 6d. *Special Edition* on Green Paper for Persons with Weak Eyesight. 2s.

Lessons in Our Laws; or, Talks at Broadacre Farm. By H. F. LESTER, B.A. Parts I. and II., 1s. 6d. each.

Little Folks' History of England. Illustrated. 1s. 6d.

Making of the Home, The. By Mrs. SAMUEL A. BARNETT. 1s. 6d.

Marlborough Books:—Arithmetic Examples, 3s. French Exercises, 3s. 6d. French Grammar, 2s. 6d. German Grammar, 3s. 6d.

Mechanics and Machine Design, Numerical Examples in Practical. By R. G. BLAINE, M.E. *New Edition, Revised and Enlarged.* With 79 Illustrations. Cloth, 2s. 6d.

Mechanics for Young Beginners, A First Book of. By the Rev. J. G. EASTON, M.A. 4s. 6d.

Selections from Cassell & Company's Publications.

Natural History Coloured Wall Sheets, Cassell's New. 17 Subjects. Size 39 by 31 in. Mounted on rollers and varnished. 3s. each.

Object Lessons from Nature. By Prof. L. C. MIALL, F.L.S. Fully Illustrated. *New and Enlarged Edition.* Two Vols., 1s. 6d. each.

Physiology for Schools. By A. T. SCHOFIELD, M.D., M.R.C.S., &c. Illustrated. Cloth, 1s. 9d.; Three Parts, paper covers, 5d. each; or cloth limp, 6d. each.

Poetry Readers, Cassell's New. Illustrated. 12 Books, 1d. each; or complete in one Vol., cloth, 1s. 6d.

Popular Educator, Cassell's NEW. With Revised Text, New Maps, New Coloured Plates, New Type, &c. In 8 Vols., 5s. each; or in Four Vols., half-morocco, 50s. the set.

Readers, Cassell's "Belle Sauvage." An entirely New Series. Fully Illustrated. Strongly bound in cloth. (*List on application.*)

Readers, Cassell's "Higher Class." (*List on application.*)

Readers, Cassell's Readable. Illustrated. (*List on application.*)

Readers for Infant Schools, Coloured. Three Books. 4d. each.

Reader, The Citizen. By H. O. ARNOLD-FORSTER, M.P. Illustrated. 1s. 6d. Also a *Scottish Edition,* cloth, 1s. 6d.

Reader, The Temperance. By Rev. J. DENNIS HIRD. 1s. 6d.

Readers, Geographical, Cassell's New. With numerous Illustrations. (*List on application.*)

Readers, The "Modern School" Geographical. (*List on application.*)

Readers, The "Modern School." Illustrated. (*List on application.*)

Reckoning, Howard's Art of. By C. FRUSHER HOWARD. Paper covers, 1s.; cloth, 2s. *New Edition,* 5s.

Round the Empire. By G. R. PARKIN. Fully Illustrated. 1s. 6d.

Science Applied to Work. By J. A. BOWER. 1s.

Science of Everyday Life. By J. A. BOWER. Illustrated. 1s.

Shade from Models, Common Objects, and Casts of Ornament, How to. By W. E. SPARKES. With 25 Plates by the Author. 3s.

Shakspere's Plays for School Use. 9 Books. Illustrated. 6d. each.

Spelling, A Complete Manual of. By J. D. MORELL, LL.D. 1s.

Technical Manuals, Cassell's. Illustrated throughout:—
Handrailing and Staircasing, 3s. 6d.—Bricklayers, Drawing for, 3s.—Building Construction, 2s.—Cabinet-Makers, Drawing for, 3s.—Carpenters and Joiners, Drawing for, 3s. 6d.—Gothic Stonework, 3s.—Linear Drawing and Practical Geometry, 2s.—Linear Drawing and Projection. The Two Vols. in One, 3s. 6d.—Machinists and Engineers, Drawing for, 4s. 6d.—Metal-Plate Workers, Drawing for, 3s.—Model Drawing, 3s.—Orthographical and Isometrical Projection, 2s.—Practical Perspective, 3s.—Stonemasons, Drawing for, 3s.—Applied Mechanics, by Sir R. S. Ball, LL.D., 2s.—Systematic Drawing and Shading, 2s.

Technical Educator, Cassell's New. With Coloured Plates and Engravings. Complete in Six Volumes, 5s. each.

Technology, Manuals of. Edited by Prof. AYRTON, F.R.S., and RICHARD WORMELL, D.Sc., M.A. Illustrated throughout:—
The Dyeing of Textile Fabrics, by Prof. Hummel, 5s.—Watch and Clock Making, by D. Glasgow, Vice-President of the British Horological Institute, 4s. 6d.—Steel and Iron, by Prof. W. H. Greenwood, F.C.S., M.I.C.E., &c., 5s.—Spinning Woollen and Worsted, by W. S. B. McLaren, M.P., 4s. 6d.—Design in Textile Fabrics, by T. R. Ashenhurst, 4s. 6d.—Practical Mechanics, by Prof. Perry, M.E., 3s. 6d.—Cutting Tools Worked by Hand and Machine, by Prof. Smith, 3s. 6d.

Things New and Old; or, Stories from English History. By H. O. ARNOLD-FORSTER, M.P. Fully Illustrated, and strongly bound in Cloth. Standards I. & II., 9d. each; Standard III., 1s.; Standard IV., 1s. 3d.; Standards V., VI., & VII., 1s. 6d. each.

This World of Ours. By H. O. ARNOLD-FORSTER, M.P. Illustrated. 3s. 6d.

Selections from Cassell & Company's Publications.

Books for Young People.

"**Little Folks**" **Half-Yearly Volume.** Containing 432 4to pages, with about 200 Illustrations, and Pictures in Colour. Boards, 3s. 6d.; cloth, 5s.

Bo-Peep. A Book for the Little Ones. With Original Stories and Verses. Illustrated throughout. Yearly Volume. Boards, 2s. 6d.; cloth, 3s. 6d.

Beneath the Banner. Being Narratives of Noble Lives and Brave Deeds. By F. J. CROSS. Illustrated. Limp cloth, 1s. Cloth gilt, 2s.

Good Morning! Good Night! By F. J. CROSS. Illustrated. Limp cloth, 1s., or cloth boards, gilt lettered, 2s.

Five Stars in a Little Pool. By EDITH CARRINGTON. Illustrated. 6s.

The Cost of a Mistake. By SARAH PITT. Illustrated. *New Edition.* 2s. 6d.

Beyond the Blue Mountains. By L. T. MEADE. 5s.

The Peep of Day. *Cassell's Illustrated Edition.* 2s. 6d.

Maggie Steele's Diary. By E. A. DILLWYN. 2s. 6d.

A Book of Merry Tales. By MAGGIE BROWNE, "SHEILA," ISABEL WILSON, and C. L. MATÉAUX. Illustrated. 3s. 6d.

A Sunday Story-Book. By MAGGIE BROWNE, SAM BROWNE, and AUNT ETHEL. Illustrated. 3s. 6d.

A Bundle of Tales. By MAGGIE BROWNE (Author of "Wanted—a King," &c.), SAM BROWNE, and AUNT ETHEL. 3s. 6d.

Pleasant Work for Busy Fingers. By MAGGIE BROWNE. Illustrated. 5s.

Born a King. By FRANCES and MARY ARNOLD-FORSTER. (The Life of Alfonso XIII., the Boy King of Spain.) Illustrated. 1s.

Cassell's Pictorial Scrap Book. Six Vols. 3s. 6d. each.

Schoolroom and Home Theatricals. By ARTHUR WAUGH. Illustrated. *New Edition.* Paper, 1s. Cloth, 1s. 6d.

Magic at Home. By Prof. HOFFMAN. Illustrated. Cloth gilt, 3s. 6d.

Little Mother Bunch. By Mrs. MOLESWORTH. Illustrated. *New Edition.* Cloth. 2s. 6d.

Heroes of Every-day Life. By LAURA LANE. With about 20 Full-page Illustrations. Cloth. 2s. 6d.

Bob Lovell's Career. By EDWARD S. ELLIS. 5s.

Books for Young People. *Cheap Edition.* Illustrated. Cloth gilt, 3s. 6d. each.

- The Champion of Odin; or, Viking Life in the Days of Old. By J. Fred. Hodgetts.
- Bound by a Spell; or, The Hunted Witch of the Forest. By the Hon. Mrs. Greene.
- Under Bayard's Banner. By Henry Frith.

Books for Young People. Illustrated. 3s. 6d. each.

- Told Out of School. By A. J. Daniels.
- Red Rose and Tiger Lily. By L. T. Meade.
- The Romance of Invention. By James Burnley.
- *Bashful Fifteen. By L. T. Meade.
- *The White House at Inch Gow. By Mrs. Pitt.
- *A Sweet Girl Graduate. By L. T. Meade.
- The King's Command: A Story for Girls. By Maggie Symington.
- *The Palace Beautiful. By L. T. Meade.
- *Polly: A New-Fashioned Girl. By L. T. Meade.
- "Follow My Leader." By Talbot Baines Reed.
- *A World of Girls: The Story of a School. By L. T. Meade.
- Lost among White Africans. By David Ker.
- For Fortune and Glory: A Story of the Soudan War. By Lewis Hough.

**Also procurable in superior binding, 5s. each.*

Selections from Cassell & Company's Publications.

"Peeps Abroad" Library. *Cheap Editions.* Gilt edges, 2s. 6d. each.

Rambles Round London. By C. L. Matéaux. Illustrated.
Around and About Old England. By C. L. Matéaux. Illustrated.
Paws and Claws. By one of the Authors of "Poems written for a Child." Illustrated.
Decisive Events in History. By Thomas Archer. With Original Illustrations.
The True Robinson Crusoes. Cloth gilt.
Peeps Abroad for Folks at Home. Illustrated throughout.
Wild Adventures in Wild Places. By Dr. Gordon Stables, R.N. Illustrated.
Modern Explorers. By Thomas Frost. Illustrated. *New and Cheaper Edition.*
Early Explorers. By Thomas Frost.
Home Chat with our Young Folks. Illustrated throughout.
Jungle, Peak, and Plain. Illustrated throughout.

The "Cross and Crown" Series. Illustrated. 2s. 6d. each.

Freedom's Sword: A Story of the Days of Wallace and Bruce. By Annie S. Swan.
Strong to Suffer: A Story of the Jews. By E. Wynne.
Heroes of the Indian Empire; or, Stories of Valour and Victory. By Ernest Foster.
In Letters of Flame: A Story of the Waldenses. By C. L. Matéaux.
Through Trial to Triumph. By Madeline B. Hunt.
By Fire and Sword: A Story of the Huguenots. By Thomas Archer.
Adam Hepburn's Vow: A Tale of Kirk and Covenant. By Annie S. Swan.
No. XIII.; or, The Story of the Lost Vestal. A Tale of Early Christian Days. By Emma Marshall.

"Golden Mottoes" Series, The. Each Book containing 208 pages, with Four full-page Original Illustrations. Crown 8vo, cloth gilt, 2s. each.

"Nil Desperandum." By the Rev. F. Langbridge, M.A.
"Bear and Forbear." By Sarah Pitt.
"Foremost if I Can." By Helen Atteridge.
"Honour is my Guide." By Jeanie Hering (Mrs. Adams-Acton).
"Aim at a Sure End." By Emily Searchfield.
"He Conquers who Endures." By the Author of "May Cunningham's Trial," &c.

Cassell's Picture Story Books. Each containing about Sixty Pages of Pictures and Stories, &c. 6d. each.

Little Talks.
Bright Stars.
Nursery Toys.
Pet's Posy.
Tiny Tales.
Daisy's Story Book.
Dot's Story Book.
A Nest of Stories.
Good-Night Stories.
Chats for Small Chatterers.
Auntie's Stories.
Birdie's Story Book.
Little Chimes.
A Sheaf of Tales.
Dewdrop Stories.

Illustrated Books for the Little Ones. Containing interesting Stories. All Illustrated. 1s. each; cloth gilt, 1s. 6d.

Bright Tales & Funny Pictures.
Merry Little Tales.
Little Tales for Little People.
Little People and Their Pets.
Tales Told for Sunday.
Sunday Stories for Small People.
Stories and Pictures for Sunday.
Bible Pictures for Boys and Girls.
Firelight Stories.
Sunlight and Shade.
Rub-a-Dub Tales.
Fine Feathers and Fluffy Fur.
Scrambles and Scrapes.
Tittle Tattle Tales.
Up and Down the Garden.
All Sorts of Adventures.
Our Sunday Stories.
Our Holiday Hours.
Indoors and Out.
Some Farm Friends.
Wandering Ways.
Dumb Friends.
Those Golden Sands.
Little Mothers & their Children.
Our Pretty Pets.
Our Schoolday Hours.
Creatures Tame.
Creatures Wild.

Selections from Cassell & Company's Publications.

Cassell's Shilling Story Books. All Illustrated, and containing Interesting Stories.

- Bunty and the Boys.
- The Heir of Elmdale.
- The Mystery at Shoncliff School.
- Claimed at Last, & Roy's Reward.
- Thorns and Tangles.
- The Cuckoo in the Robin's Nest.
- John's Mistake. [Pitchers.
- The History of Five Little Diamonds in the Sand.
- Surly Bob.
- The Giant's Cradle.
- Shag and Doll.
- Aunt Lucia's Locket.
- The Magic Mirror.
- The Cost of Revenge.
- Clever Frank.
- Among the Redskins.
- The Ferryman of Brill.
- Harry Maxwell.
- A Banished Monarch.
- Seventeen Cats.

"Wanted—a King" Series. *Cheap Edition.* Illustrated. 2s. 6d. each.
- Great Grandmamma. By Georgina M. Synge.
- Robin's Ride. By Ellinor Davenport Adams.
- Wanted—a King; or, How Merle set the Nursery Rhymes to Rights. By Maggie Browne. With Original Designs by Harry Furniss.
- Fairy Tales in Other Lands. By Julia Goddard.

The World's Workers. A Series of New and Original Volumes. With Portraits printed on a tint as Frontispiece. 1s. each.

- John Cassell. By G. Holden Pike.
- Charles Haddon Spurgeon. By G. Holden Pike.
- Dr. Arnold of Rugby. By Rose E. Selfe.
- The Earl of Shaftesbury. By Henry Frith.
- Sarah Robinson, Agnes Weston, and Mrs. Meredith. By E. M. Tomkinson.
- Thomas A. Edison and Samuel F. B. Morse. By Dr. Denslow and J. Marsh Parker.
- Mrs. Somerville and Mary Carpenter. By Phyllis Browne.
- General Gordon. By the Rev. S. A. Swaine.
- Charles Dickens. By his Eldest Daughter.
- Sir Titus Salt and George Moore. By J. Burnley.
- Florence Nightingale, Catherine Marsh, Frances Ridley Havergal, Mrs. Ranyard ("L. N. R."). By Lizzie Alldridge.
- Dr. Guthrie, Father Mathew, Elihu Burritt, George Livesey. By John W. Kirton, LL.D.
- Sir Henry Havelock and Colin Campbell Lord Clyde. By E. C. Phillips.
- Abraham Lincoln. By Ernest Foster.
- George Müller and Andrew Reed. By E. R. Pitman.
- Richard Cobden. By R. Gowing.
- Benjamin Franklin. By E. M. Tomkinson.
- Handel. By Eliza Clarke. [Swaine.
- Turner the Artist. By the Rev. S. A.
- George and Robert Stephenson. By C. L. Matéaux.
- David Livingstone. By Robert Smiles.

*** *The above Works can also be had Three in One Vol., cloth, gilt edges, 3s.*

Library of Wonders. Illustrated Gift-books for Boys. Paper, 1s.; cloth, 1s. 6d.
- Wonderful Balloon Ascents.
- Wonderful Adventures.
- Wonderful Escapes.
- Wonders of Animal Instinct.
- Wonders of Bodily Strength and Skill.

Cassell's Eighteenpenny Story Books. Illustrated.
- Wee Willie Winkie.
- Ups and Downs of a Donkey's Life.
- Three Wee Ulster Lassies.
- Up the Ladder.
- Dick's Hero; and other Stories.
- The Chip Boy.
- Raggles, Baggles, and the Emperor.
- Roses from Thorns.
- Faith's Father.
- By Land and Sea.
- The Young Berringtons.
- Jeff and Leff.
- Tom Morris's Error.
- Worth more than Gold.
- "Through Flood—Through Fire;" and other Stories.
- The Girl with the Golden Locks.
- Stories of the Olden Time.

Gift Books for Young People. By Popular Authors. With Four Original Illustrations in each. Cloth gilt, 1s. 6d. each.

- The Boy Hunters of Kentucky. By Edward S. Ellis.
- Red Feather: a Tale of the American Frontier. By Edward S. Ellis.
- Seeking a City.
- Rhoda's Reward; or, "If Wishes were Horses."
- Jack Marston's Anchor.
- Frank's Life-Battle; or, The Three Friends.
- Fritters. By Sarah Pitt.
- The Two Hardcastles. By Madeline Bonavia Hunt.
- Major Monk's Motto. By the Rev. F. Langbridge.
- Trixy. By Maggie Symington.
- Rags and Rainbows: A Story of Thanksgiving.
- Uncle William's Charges; or, The Broken Trust.
- Pretty Pink's Purpose; or, The Little Street Merchants.
- Tim Thomson's Trial. By George Weatherly.
- Ursula's Stumbling-Block. By Julia Goddard.
- Ruth's Life-Work. By the Rev. Joseph Johnson.

Selections from Cassell & Company's Publications.

Cassell's Two-Shilling Story Books. Illustrated.

- Margaret's Enemy.
- Stories of the Tower.
- Mr. Burke's Nieces.
- May Cunningham's Trial.
- The Top of the Ladder: How to Reach it.
- Little Flotsam.
- Madge and Her Friends.
- The Children of the Court.
- Maid Marjory.
- Peggy, and other Tales.
- The Four Cats of the Tippertons.
- Marion's Two Homes.
- Little Folks' Sunday Book.
- Two Fourpenny Bits.
- Poor Nelly.
- Tom Heriot.
- Through Peril to Fortune.
- Aunt Tabitha's Waifs.
- In Mischief Again.

Cheap Editions of Popular Volumes for Young People. Bound in cloth, gilt edges, 2s. 6d. each.

- In Quest of Gold; or, Under the Whanga Falls.
- On Board the *Esmeralda*; or, Martin Leigh's Log.
- For Queen and King.
- Esther West.
- Three Homes.
- Working to Win.
- Perils Afloat and Brigands Ashore.

Books by Edward S. Ellis. Illustrated. Cloth, 2s. 6d. each.

- The Great Cattle Trail.
- The Path in the Ravine.
- The Young Ranchers.
- The Hunters of the Ozark.
- The Camp in the Mountains.
- Ned in the Woods. A Tale of Early Days in the West.
- Down the Mississippi.
- The Last War Trail.
- Ned on the River. A Tale of Indian River Warfare.
- Footprints in the Forest.
- Up the Tapajos.
- Ned in the Block House. A Story of Pioneer Life in Kentucky.
- The Lost Trail.
- Camp-Fire and Wigwam.
- Lost in the Wilds.
- Lost in Samoa. A Tale of Adventure in the Navigator Islands.
- Tad; or, "Getting Even" with Him.

The "World in Pictures." Illustrated throughout. *Cheap Edition.* 1s. 6d. each.

- A Ramble Round France.
- All the Russias.
- Chats about Germany.
- The Eastern Wonderland (Japan).
- Glimpses of South America.
- Round Africa.
- The Land of Temples (India).
- The Isles of the Pacific.
- Peeps into China
- The Land of Pyramids (Egypt).

Half-Crown Story Books.

- Pictures of School Life and Boyhood.
- Pen's Perplexities.
- At the South Pole.

Books for the Little Ones.

- Rhymes for the Young Folk. By William Allingham. Beautifully Illustrated. 3s. 6d.
- The History Scrap Book. With nearly 1,000 Engravings. Cloth, 7s. 6d.
- The Sunday Scrap Book. With Several Hundred Illustrations. Paper boards, 3s. 6d.; cloth, gilt edges, 5s.
- The Old Fairy Tales. With Original Illustrations. Boards, 1s.; cloth, 1s. 6d.

Albums for Children. 3s. 6d. each.

- The Album for Home, School, and Play. Containing Stories by Popular Authors. Illustrated.
- My Own Album of Animals. With Full-page Illustrations.
- Picture Album of All Sorts. With Full-page Illustrations.
- The Chit-Chat Album. Illustrated throughout.

Cassell & Company's Complete Catalogue *will be sent post free on application to*

CASSELL & COMPANY, Limited, *Ludgate Hill, London.*

www.ingramcontent.com/pod-product-compliance
Lightning Source LLC
Chambersburg PA
CBHW080436110426
42743CB00016B/3185